Choice Architecture

From Vitruvius in the 1st century BCE on, there has been an attempt to understand how architecture works, especially in its poetic aspect but also in its basic functions. Design can encourage us to walk, to experience community, to imagine new ways of being, and can affect countless other choices we make that shape our health and happiness.

Using the ideas of rational choice theory and behavioral economics, *Choice Architecture* shows how behavior, design, and wellness are deeply interconnected. As active agents, we choose our responses to the architectural meanings we encounter based on our perception of our individual contexts. The book offers a way to approach the design of spaces for human flourishing and explains in rich detail how the potential of the built environment to influence our well-being can be realized.

Avani Parikh is an architect planner with a consulting practice in healthcare architecture. She was co-chair of the AIANY Health Facilities Committee and has also served on various nonprofit and government committees in New York and Mumbai, formulating an innovative Transfer of Development Rights proposal for Bombay's Development Plan. She has written about and taught modern architecture, city planning, and the history and theory of healthcare design.

Prashant Parikh was a Senior Research Scholar at the University of Pennsylvania and Stanford University. Now an independent scholar, he is a pioneer in the application of game theory to communication and meaning, and the author of three books on philosophical and linguistic semantics including *Language and Equilibrium*.

Choice Architecture

A New Approach to Behavior,
Design, and Wellness

Avani Parikh and Prashant Parikh

Routledge
Taylor & Francis Group

NEW YORK AND LONDON

First published 2018
by Routledge
711 Third Avenue, New York, NY 10017

and by Routledge
2 Park Square, Milton Park, Abingdon, Oxon, OX14 4RN

Routledge is an imprint of the Taylor & Francis Group, an informa business

Library of Congress Cataloging-in-Publication Data
A catalog record for this book has been requested

ISBN: 978-0-8153-7051-2 (hbk)
ISBN: 978-1-351-24899-0 (ebk)

Typeset in Times New Roman
by Apex CoVantage, LLC

For our son Neal

Contents

Figures

Acknowledgments

We would like to thank David Burney, Arindam Dutta, Debajyoti Pati, and Richard Thomas for their helpful comments on the book. We are also grateful to Harry Mallgrave for his interest in our project. Many others, too, such as John Eberhard, Kenneth Frampton, Pelle Guldborg Hansen, Charlie Hecht, Richard Jackson, Tom Jung, Rahul Mehrotra, Bimal Patel, Ray Pentecost, Judy Raymo, Wayne Ruga, Yehuda Safran, and Suhrud Sardesai supported the project in other ways. Mark Patrizio provided drawings that visually capture what we have conveyed in words and numbers. Katharine Maller, our architecture editor at Routledge, has been simply super.

The main title of our book, "Choice Architecture," has been drawn from Chapter 5 of Thaler and Sunstein's wonderful book *Nudge*, although they use the term much more broadly than we do.

Preface

Choice Architecture: A New Approach to Behavior, Design, and Wellness offers a new way to explain how architecture affects human well-being. It is the first study to use the seminal ideas of rational choice theory and behavioral economics to explore how architects can nudge people toward healthy action through the built environment. The insights from this model of human behavior into how architecture works and into how it can address issues of health are fresh and deep and go beyond various existing approaches such as phenomenology, Gibsonian psychology, systems theory, evidence-based design, and others. It is an interdisciplinary book at the intersection of architecture, economics and psychology, and health.

The key concept that mediates the relationship between architecture and health is experience and the key determining component of experience is human choice. People are active agents rather than passive experiencers and what they experience is the result of conscious or unconscious choices based partly on the built environment in which they find themselves.

The Western paradigm for choice has always privileged rational action but recent behavioral findings inaugurated by the psychologists Amos Tversky and Daniel Kahneman have clarified various additional subtle factors that affect how we choose. A combination of the two models of rational and irrational behavior enables us to develop an explanatory and predictive framework we call *choice architecture*.

While the consequences of the framework are broad and encompass health and wellness in various ways, the book's focus is on introducing its potential with simple illustrative examples that demonstrate its range and power. The book is presented in four chapters as listed in the table of contents.

The opening chapter describes briefly how architecture surrounds us even if we do not often notice its effect on us. The field of design and health has existed for over half a century to promote wellness through architecture. As chronic lifestyle diseases have proliferated, it has now acquired a practical urgency even though it has yet to have a significant impact. There are probably two reasons for this. One is that while much evidence of the link between our environment and our health has been gathered, the field has yet to create a satisfying theoretical perspective that can inform this data. We hope to contribute to this effort and we show that our architectural experiences are far from simple and have an intricate structure capable of open-ended articulation. The second reason is that architects in the main view the field's contributions as external and not quite integrated into its very language. This is also part of what we attempt, to show how choice theory enables one to include wellness in design in an internal rather than merely external way.

The book does not address the larger non-built physical environment—factors like noise, pollution, disease—but the *design* potential of the built environment. As important to wellness is the socioeconomic environment, especially the presence of poverty, but architectural initiatives are limited in their power to affect such things and we do not discuss them here.

In the next chapter, we describe our new framework. Certain aspects of the relationship between design and health are obvious. For example, doors in interior spaces may serve the basic function of exits to natural vistas and gardens, or windows may provide views that are life-enhancing. But most aspects of the built environment are not so readily comprehensible. Subtler thinking is required and this involves constructing a theoretical framework.

Choice theory is the study of decision-making in a variety of situations. We apply it in a novel way to architectural experience and include choices that are both rational and irrational. In addition, we provide a new way of thinking about architectural meaning. The core idea in combining rational and irrational choice theory with an account of architectural meaning is that it is the particular human *interpretations* of the built environment that result in one type of action or another and lead to positive or negative effects on our health. The whole treatment is elementary and requires no more than arithmetic to understand. It is also done via a hypothetical character named Phil who chooses between actions like walking and taking the bus to make the more abstract considerations easy to grasp.

In the majority of decisions we make, we are consistently rational. But surprisingly often we are irrational.

We devote the bulk of the third chapter to understanding irrationality and exploring several different ways in which we can be irrational. We discuss them from architectural vantage points partly by constructing analogies with similar situations in other domains. An interesting feature of our investigation is that we show how irrationality can be turned to our advantage.

The principles of behavioral economics discussed are anchoring, availability, zero cost, nonlinearity, representativeness, framing, and shifting reference points. Again, these principles are discussed via examples in a wide range of architectural settings such as streets, workplaces, neighborhoods, public plazas, playgrounds, doctors' clinics, and interiors, and involve no more than arithmetical knowledge.

The concluding chapter is more reflective. It discusses the consequences of our approach for architecture, in particular for the Vitruvian triad of utility, firmness, and beauty, and its connection to health and wellness. It also considers possible problems with our approach such as modeling human behavior via mathematics in a humanistic area and the possible dangers of social engineering. Overall, our method enables the meeting of science and design and could result in the field becoming more scientific while retaining the subtler dimensions of meaning, aesthetics, and experience that are central to architecture. We show how health and wellness are an integral part of the built environment because architecture is never neutral: it will always have either a positive or negative effect on our health.

By combining choice theory with a theory of architectural meaning and interpretation, we show how our approach can be unified with mainstream architectural approaches both in theory and in practice. We argue that health is not external to the other functions architecture serves and is fully part of the Vitruvian triad which is as fundamental to architecture as the Hippocratic oath is to medicine.

1 The Inescapable Architecture of Everyday Life

Architecture surrounds us but there is little general awareness of its impact on us. A mother once spoke about selecting a school for her daughter and she said that most of the institutions she visited had buildings that seemed more like prisons. She wondered how being schooled in a rigid corridor-centric building without art or natural light could make a child bright, courageous, and well-rounded with an appreciation for beauty in life.

Indeed, not just schools but the entire built environment plays a major role in all our lives and has the potential to provide a framework for our flourishing. Streets we walk on, rooms we work in, even corridors we go through all affect us in myriad ways. Most of us give these spaces no more than a passing thought. In *An Outline of European Architecture*, the architectural historian Nikolaus Pevsner said that "a bicycle shed is a building; Lincoln Cathedral is a piece of architecture."[1] The implicit assumption he made—and we all make—is that the bicycle shed is unimportant and has nothing to offer us. We tend to notice only what is striking or dramatic, in a word, monumental, and the everyday environment which is relatively humdrum escapes our gaze.

This is a natural corollary of the inaccessibility of the everyday in a wider sense. Ordinary moments like sipping a cup of morning coffee elapse unremembered; only the extraordinary persists. It takes effort to turn our attention to daily matters because we are generally able to manage them unconsciously. When we do, a very rich structure reveals itself.

Not long ago, the novelist David Foster Wallace narrated the following story in a commencement speech: "There are these two young fish swimming along and they happen to meet an older fish swimming the other way, who nods at them and says 'Morning, boys. How's the water?' And the two young fish swim on for a bit, and then eventually one of them looks over at the other and goes 'What the hell is water?'" Wallace adds, "The immediate point of the fish story is that the most obvious, ubiquitous, important realities are often the ones that are the hardest to see and talk about."

Architecture is like this ambient water. It is invisible but inescapable. The trace each encounter with it leaves on us is infinitesimal, but an infinity of such imperceptible experiences over the course of days, months, years can and do add up. The macro impacts of these micro effects go unremarked unless there is some breakdown or disaster in our dwellings. As a result, they remain mute enclosures that are poorly understood. Perhaps the most important aspect of our ordinary surroundings is how they affect our well-being.

The field of design and health emerged in the previous mid-century to study the effects of the built environment and to recommend ways to promote wellness through architecture. With the unfortunate growth of lifestyle diseases, it has now acquired a practical urgency even though it has yet to have a wider impact. One reason for this may be that while a great deal of convincing evidence has been accumulated leading to many practical initiatives, the field has yet to forge a unifying theoretical perspective that can interpret this data, explain it, and even make new and unexpected predictions. We hope to contribute to this effort, especially to show that our architectural interactions are far from obvious and possess a deep and fascinating structure capable of endless elaboration.

There are many levels at which this immersive built environment exerts its influence. It can be as simple as a single enclosure such as a room or Pevsner's bicycle shed. It can accommodate multiple such spaces in apartments and offices. The latter constitute complex multistory buildings including soaring monuments. Less easily grasped are neighborhoods and cities. Beyond these lie entire regions connected by geography and transportation networks. How these levels are designed and linked to each other and the meanings they generate have a lasting impact.

The user is in fact an active rather than passive agent and participates in shaping his experience and his response to the architecture he encounters. By using very recent ideas from economics and psychology that deal with how people make choices, we build a framework that provides a way to understand architecture and how it affects our health. Our protagonist is a genial character named Phil who occasionally along with his neighbor Tom negotiates different choices of actions involving physical activity, social interaction, and emotions that result in a wide range of types of effects on health, each experienced through varied architectural elements such as streets, stairways, workplaces, residential neighborhoods, public plazas, parks and playgrounds, and so on. The basic focus throughout the book is on human behavior in the context of design that affects Phil's wellness—and by implication ours—positively or negatively, in big ways or small.

This framework is developed in detail and some of the basic concepts of choice theory, a basic framework of ideas in economics, are introduced and related to architectural meaning. The examples allow us to draw out the abstract ideas from the concrete settings. A key pair of distinctions helps us understand this diverse terrain of action. One is what economists label rational and irrational actions and the other is Daniel Kahneman's[2] slow and fast thinking. According to Kahneman, slow deliberation generally results in rational choices whereas fast intuitive thinking sometimes results in irrational choices. In the next chapter we'll explain what makes an action rational or irrational. We try to show how both kinds of choices can be turned to our advantage. The definition captures something about the logic of choosing. For example, if Phil is at a restaurant and initially feels like choosing an avocado sandwich over an egg sandwich which he prefers to a cheese sandwich, we could reasonably expect him to opt for the avocado sandwich over the cheese sandwich as well. If Phil doesn't, if he prefers the cheese sandwich to the avocado sandwich instead, we would consider the logic of his choices aberrant and call it irrational.

The way we use the terms "rational" and "irrational" is very different from both colloquial uses and other technical uses such as those of Kierkegaard, William James, and Sigmund Freud among others. If Phil enjoys skydiving every weekend, some may deem him irrational in a colloquial sense because they think he is endangering his life too much. But if he has carefully weighed the pleasure he derives from the activity against its risks then in our economic sense his choice would be rational. The philosophical senses have little to do with our distinction between rational and irrational actions. They originate in different models of the mind than ours and have different applications.

There are just a few other technical terms in this book that describe the principles underlying choice. They help to orient the reader to a new way of thinking about architecture. We also show in the last chapter that the historical Vitruvian triad of utility, firmness, and beauty that has organized architecture for two thousand years itself appears in a different light in this new context. Most important, we argue that health and wellness are an integral part of all architecture at all levels and should not be an afterthought.

We offer a way to make the invisible architectural water surrounding us visible. This framework combined with existing approaches in the field of design and health could help architects to realize the promise of our schools and other everyday places, enabling people to become bright, courageous, and well-rounded individuals with an appreciation for beauty in life.

Notes

1 Pevsner (1943/1990, p. 15).
2 Kahneman (2011).

2 A Framework for Architectural Interpretation

Ever since Vitruvius's classical treatise *The Ten Books on Architecture*, the field's essence has always lain in utility, firmness, and beauty. These dimensions have generally comprised traditional mandates such as fulfilling functions and conveying beauty via a sound structure. Since the mid to late twentieth century, they have been broadened to encompass contemporary social demands such as improving health and conserving energy as these functions have acquired a certain urgency. Someone new to this relatively recent connection between architecture and health may well wonder how one could possibly affect the other.

In this book, we offer a new framework for thinking about how architecture can contribute to our health. Certain aspects of this relationship are just common sense. For example, making interior and exterior spaces adequately lit is obviously important for basic safety. Other aspects, indeed the majority of elements of the built environment, do not yield to such straightforward thinking. Subtler considerations are involved and so a *theoretical framework* is required.

In recent years, a few theoretical approaches to architecture have been proposed, some drawing upon phenomenology[1] and Gibsonian psychology[2] and others influenced by the social sciences (e.g. systems theory, evolutionary psychology, environmental psychology, gestalt theory, etc.). There are also more practically oriented models such as evidence-based design, human factor design, and action research, but these fall short because they tend to report empirical observations and measurements without a fuller understanding of why architecture has the effects it does. What is needed is a framework that outlines a *theory* and *principles* which allow one to explain why, for example, a certain kind of street has a positive or negative effect on human well-being. Without such explanations, the field of design and health remains merely a collection of data. A combination of theory and practice can be found in recent neuroscientific advances but at the present time such studies are also likely to be more data-driven than theory-driven as too little is understood about the brain's processes (although this is obviously changing rapidly).[3]

Current theoretical frameworks such as phenomenology and Gibsonian psychology have enriched our understanding and afforded new ways of thinking about the problem. But they have certain serious shortcomings: despite an impressive philosophical lineage, the former[4] tends to be descriptive rather than explanatory, and so is likely to have different uses from the ones that interest us here, and it has proven difficult to elaborate the latter's main idea of an affordance, promising though it is, to create a satisfactory theory. It, too, tends to be more descriptive than explanatory. For example, in a recent paper[5] applying Gibson's ideas, there are detailed matrices recording many of the affordances of objects and materials, but these observations are nevertheless largely based on common sense. It is hard to see why architects would need to consult such compilations to make design decisions. More importantly, there are few if any "principles" in the applications of the theory to architecture and so there are few *insights* it is able to offer, at least in this area. We will show later how affordances are related to a concept similar to one we will use.

Perhaps the central shared idea, whether explicit or implicit, in all of these frameworks, whether theoretical or practical, is the following representation or model:

elements in the built environment → human experience → positive or negative effects on health

This says that elements in the built environment bring about human experiences and these in turn lead to positive or negative effects on our health. The arrows linking the three items can be thought of as causal connections.

As far as we know, none of the existing approaches has succeeded in making the middle term of *human experience* sufficiently concrete. As it stands, it is far too broad. An analytic orientation that breaks it down into relevant parts is needed, one that yields not just explanations but also predictions. Our framework is able to both explain and predict outcomes based on a theory of how people respond to various elements in the built environment. In a nutshell, it describes how a person *chooses* to act one way rather than another based on what his architectural encounters *mean* to him.

Our framework is drawn principally from what is called choice theory, an approach to human decision-making and action that is widespread in the social sciences, especially economics where it originated, and beyond. It is also called decision theory. It is the study of how people choose between alternative actions such as walking, biking, taking the bus, or driving. People can be rational or irrational in their decision-making behavior and in our use of choice theory we include both. The mainstream approach of neoclassical economics still focuses exclusively on rationality but the fast-growing field of behavioral economics has shown that the assumption of rational behavior gives incorrect results in many situations.[6] More recently, these ideas of rationality and irrationality have even made their way into popular writing that relates them to everyday life.[7] There is also the possibility of combining such a dual orientation with the nascent field of neuroeconomics which studies decision-making at the level of the brain and connects it with choice theory at a psychological level.

We apply these ideas from conventional and behavioral economics to architecture in a fresh way and we also add to them a new way of thinking about architectural experience and interpretation. The key idea in combining "rational and irrational choice theory" with an account of architectural meaning is that it is the particular human interpretations of the built environment conceptualized in a certain way that result in one type of action or another and in turn lead to positive or negative effects on our health. Going back to the schema above, we will use these two parts—choice theory and a framework for architectural interpretation—to show how the middle term of human experience can be analyzed.

This framework was initially summarized in a poster Avani Parikh presented at the 2011 Design and Health Seventh World Congress and Exhibition in Boston.[8] Later this work was described in two articles.[9] This book represents a fuller working out of the earlier ideas. The clearest way to present them is to develop particular examples and then show how they can be generalized.

2.1 Rational Persons

Let's say Phil is about to set off to work one spring morning. He can either walk or take the bus. These options may be compactly expressed by the set choices = {*walk, take the bus*}. What might induce him to walk, which is obviously better for his health but takes more time and effort? Many things could influence him: whether he is late for work or it is raining, whether he plans to go to the gym later in the day, and so on. But all designers and architects are likely to concur that if there are no extraneous factors, a more inviting walking experience would nudge him toward walking. Surprisingly, this is true even if Phil is not particularly aware of design and is not consciously oriented to observing his surroundings except in a perfunctory, utilitarian way. This is because the effects of the environments we move about in are largely unconscious even for those of us who are more attuned to aesthetic considerations.

Even if he had earlier decided to take the bus, upon viewing the cheerful and attractive appearance of the street, he may end up preferring to walk—other things being equal. This changed preference for walking over taking the bus may be expressed as *walk* > *take the bus* where the > sign is simply a succinct way of saying *is preferred to*. Earlier, his preference was *take the bus* > *walk*; now it has reversed. As a rational person, Phil would naturally select his most preferred option and set off on foot toward his place of work. This would have a small positive effect on his health, not only through the physical exercise he gets but also owing to the pleasing impact of the street on his mood. That is, walking affects him doubly, through exercise and through elevating his mood.

There could be other scenarios. He might have been neutral toward his choices, expressed as *walk* ~ *take the bus*, or may not have given them a thought. But once he steps out, the street could nevertheless lead him to form the same preference as before. Or he might already have the healthy preference based on his inner motivations and the street would just reinforce it.

Moreover, Phil might behave differently on different days, sometimes responding to the street and at other times not. This is because other things may not always be equal and there may be countervailing factors like his being late for work or the weather. It is likely that if a health-oriented street has the kind of effect outlined above, then, during the course of the year, he will take to walking more often than he would have, had a differently designed street experience presented itself. So the effects of design have to be averaged over a sufficiently extended time period. Not only this, they have to cover a whole community as the interest is in benefiting all the relevant people, not just Phil, and different people may differ somewhat in their circumstances and orientations. For example, we have simplified Phil's choices to just two: walk or take the bus. For other members of the community there could well be different routines, different destinations, and therefore different possibilities. Maybe some people drive to work. So the problem for designers is a difficult one as it involves the whole environment, both physical and social, and the whole community of users over an extended duration.

2.2 Architects and Designers

Assume for the time being that Phil is typical of his community. Then how should a designer tasked with designing Phil's neighborhood proceed? If her mandate is to make the neighborhood more healthful, then she should not only study its physical layout but also the habits of the community and how they use the neighborhood. Specifically, she should become aware that the people who live there face a choice between walking and taking the bus and that she could influence this choice. She would, of course, consult some predictive and explanatory framework of the kind we are articulating here.

Returning to Phil's street, faced with various alternatives for its design, she can try to anticipate how users might react to each one and thereby help in a modest way toward improving the health of a community. Similarly, she could address other aspects of the neighborhood and its uses and thereby have an even bigger positive effect.

If such an awareness were to spread through the architectural profession and were to be extended to all of the built environment, the results could be significant. They may even contribute to substantially reducing the cost of healthcare by inducing people to adopt more healthy actions that prevent the onset of illness. The flip side of this is also true: if healthy design is neglected, it could have deleterious effects. Architecture is thus seldom neutral toward health: it will generally have some effect, positive or negative. One reason why this has been ignored until recently is that each individual effect is often small, transient, and barely noticeable. Like the proverbial straw that broke the camel's back, these tiny effects can add up to tangible outcomes even across the population of an entire country. As healthcare costs have risen in recent decades, there is now much greater attention being paid to architecture's link with health.

So it is important for architects and designers to be able to predict how different designs work and to explain such effects after the fact. For this, the collection of data is certainly critical as one may extrapolate from past behavior to future behavior. If one wants greater confidence in such correlations then a full-fledged theoretical approach that provides genuine understanding of cause and effect becomes indispensable.

There is occasionally some resistance from architects who have been trained to think primarily of the third dimension of beauty from the Vitruvian triad as the only grand goal of design. They may see the demands of improving health and sustainability as not *real* architecture. This is a flawed argument. Even in designing a doorway, one has to think not only of beauty and aesthetic meaning and all those good things but also of the practical function the doorway has to serve. This has been assimilated to such a degree in the consciousness of architects that no one complains that making a door wide enough to allow comfortable passage is not real architecture. Indeed, it is just taken for granted. Why can't the same happen with health? Some may not want to go so far as to say form follows function, but isn't thinking of the effects of design on health and sustainability just an extension of such commonplace functions as doorways to more communitarian and even utopian functions?

Architecture, like all of the arts, is a deeply *communicative* process. It is two-sided. It involves not just the designer but also the user. Whether the aim is to create something beautiful or to fulfill a function, the process involves both sides. And the reason why architecture is so powerful is that it literally envelops us. This implies a great responsibility to use the means available to affect the communities for which architects design not only by occasionally stunning aesthetic achievements but equally by making the right utopian choices. This is also a unique opportunity to expand the field of creative architectural endeavors. As we will demonstrate, often the two orientations are not at odds mainly because good aesthetic decisions generally have positive effects on health.

2.3 Looking a Little More Closely at What Happens Inside Phil

Now that the stage has been set, let's examine Phil's experience more closely. Earlier, we said that the middle term of *experience* in the schema

   built environment → experience → effects on health

had been approached more holistically than analytically resulting in the explanation of the effect of the street on Phil being short-circuited: all that is left to be said is that the cheerful and attractive street has a positive effect on his mood. His options of walking and taking the bus remain untheorized, the change of preference he undergoes goes untheorized, and so his *choosing* to walk remains at best superficially observed.

Phil is an active agent, one who is constantly (if unconsciously) making choices and performing actions, whether they affect his health or not. While his experience of the street is a large whole, all we need to do is isolate its relevant aspects. We can safely ignore the rest. That is how theoretical inquiry always proceeds.

His total environment—social and physical—affords the two choices of walking or taking the bus and he is aware of these alternatives. They are part of his experience. Then, either he remains neutral toward these options or he does not think more about them, or, as we have supposed, he forms the undesired preference for taking the bus based on his tendency to opt for the easier course and his inherent inertia. Next, he steps out onto the street and is charmed by its appearance, only hazily aware of what is happening to him. It leads him to change (or form anew) his preference in favor of walking: this is how he unconsciously *interprets* the street. The alternatives

Figure 2.1 A cheerful street

he faces and the formation of a new preference or a reinforced preference is the *meaning* the street holds for him. Based on this, and being rational, he selects his favored action, namely walking, and proceeds to walk. This decision has a positive effect on him overall.

Thus, a holistic experience can be broken down into relevant components in the following way:

experience: ({*walk, take the bus*}, {*walk* > *bus*}) → *walk*

That is, the analyzed experience is just the choices and preferences and the ensuing action. Putting this slightly more abstractly:

experience: (choices, preferences) → action

Here "preferences" refers to his entire set of preferences. In Phil's case there is just the single preference for walking over taking the bus but in other situations there may be other actions and therefore other preferences as well. This slice of Phil's experience can then be inserted into the whole schema as follows:

built environment → [(choices, preferences) → action] → effects on   health

Again, the part within the square brackets is just the relevant aspect of experience shorn of all the stuff that can be ignored. In particular, we are setting aside the obvious impact of the dazzling street on Phil, something that often gets identified with his experience, and are digging deeper into the internal consequences of this impact.

From this, we can say that for our purposes Phil's interpretation of the environment is just this experience boiled down to its essentials. That is, we can define:

meaning of street = ({*walk, take the bus*}, {*walk* ≻ *bus*})

And, more abstractly:

meaning of built environment = (choices, preferences)

These specifications of meaning are stipulated and in so doing we are introducing a new way to think about architectural interpretation. It allows us to write:

built environment → meaning → action → effects on health

In other words, the built environment is interpreted by Phil as having a meaning, which leads him to act in a certain way, and this has an effect on his health.

Meaning in architecture and elsewhere is a rich and multifaceted thing. The street certainly holds other meanings. For example, it may say something about the prosperity of the community or even something recondite about the nature of contemporary cities. While such other meanings are rightly of great interest to architects and designers, they are not of direct interest here even if such meanings have a positive effect on Phil's health. It may be that the street reminds Phil he belongs to a well-off community and this makes him feel good, or that he is a reflective man and it leads him to contemplate the nature of contemporary cities over many happy hours. For our purposes, these are relatively incidental and passing pleasures and are not easily generalizable and incorporable in a *theory* of architecture and health.

The scene could also engage Phil purely aesthetically via its pleasing proportions and layout, its tree-lined streetscape, and its lively ambience. This aesthetic meaning helps to generate the salubrious meaning above. That is, beauty has two kinds of effects—direct and indirect—and what is relevant in this framework is its indirect effects. So we will not include it directly in the kind of meaning that matters here though it will always be present in the background.

In the framework of architectural interpretation we are advancing, meaning is just the choices and preferences taken together as a single entity that we will describe later. We have identified the meaning of the street with a slice of Phil's experience, and, since his experience changes from day to day, so will the meaning. When external factors do enter his calculus, the street will no longer hold this meaning, and may even be meaningless from this perspective as he may ignore it altogether. In this framework, meaning and interpretation are variable things, "negotiated" afresh on every encounter even with the very same element in the built environment.

This is not always the most appropriate definition of meaning. When an architect designs a building, for example, and its wider interpretations have to be considered, then it makes more sense to maintain a relatively static notion of meaning as we do not want it identified with what goes on in people's heads but rather with the more objective elements of the design itself which do not change from person to person or from day to day. In our situation the more subjective account is a better one as it allows us to track its variations through time and thereby its overall effect on the health of a community. This can also be expressed differently by saying that in the first case it is the physical and socio-historical context that matters and that in the second case it is the mental context that matters. As the physical context is obviously more or less fixed, the meaning it confers does not change much in a particular period,[10] whereas as the mental context is highly variable, the meaning it confers changes a great deal.

The definition of meaning we have chosen provides a natural way to connect the traditional concerns of utility, firmness, and beauty with choice theory. The latter fits snugly into the built environment when it is seen as constituting its meaning and does not seem like a deus ex machina. Moreover, this choice-theoretic meaning offers a credible bridge between architecture and action that has otherwise seemed elusive and forced, especially in the kind of utopian context we are considering.

We are not yet done with Phil. The framework of interpretation and effect we have so far described informally is just the bare bones of what is needed for a full explanation. The alert reader will have realized that we have merely claimed that:

cheerful street → preference for walking

and by implication that:

depressing street → preference for taking the bus

but there is no explanation of these crucial facts. How can one explain that the influences aren't switched around, that a depressing street leads to walking and a cheerful street to taking the bus? Merely saying that cheerfulness

Figure 2.2 A depressing street

is inviting begs the question. But almost all the descriptive frameworks, whether data-driven or theory-driven, reiterate this observation as far as we can determine. This is part of the reason why they fall short. We have at least been able to describe Phil as an active agent by focusing relatively precisely on some key aspects of his experience that determine his decision to walk. This is a good beginning but it is still just a sketch. A crucial gap remains to be filled. The part we have outlined is called rational choice theory in the social sciences, especially economics, and this is combined with a new definition of architectural meaning. We first want to consolidate the sketch itself by developing the ideas a little more abstractly and, in addition, describing how the choices are formed and how the actual action is selected. This will lead naturally to completing the explanation of why it is the cheerful and attractive street that prompts Phil to walk and not the other way around.

2.4 Abstracting From Phil: The Elements of Choice Theory

There are three basic elements that make up rational choice theory: choice sets, preferences, and rationality.

Choice Sets

The starting point for our description of how Phil chooses to walk was the choices he faces. This was the set choices = choices(Phil) = {*walk, take the bus*}.[11] If it had been Tom, Phil's neighbor, his options may have been choices(Tom) = {*walk, take the bus, drive*} because Tom owns a car and sometimes drives to work. There are two questions that arise here as we begin to think more abstractly about how an agent makes a choice. The first is: how do we represent such actions in a more general way? And the second is: where do these actions come from?

In a general setting, there may be all kinds of possible actions that an agent can choose from and we may not want to get bogged down with finding a descriptive word for each one. In such cases, we can just label them *a, b, c. . . .*, or $a_1, a_2, a_3, . . ., a_n$ to avoid running out of letters, although we will never need to consider too many actions all at once in this book. These may then be collected into an agent's choice set. This can be written choices = {$a_1, a_2, a_3, . . ., a_n$} or if the choice set is called C we could write $C = \{a_1, a_2, a_3, . . ., a_n\}$. This is nothing but a general analogue of Phil's choice set choices = {*walk, take the bus*}. We are not going to actually need such an impersonal representation often but it is useful to know that Phil's twofold choices and Tom's threefold choices can be extended in a natural way to other environments where an agent may have different and many more choices. Occasionally we will need to refer to an arbitrary element in a choice set. For this we will use the variables $x, y,$ and z. The first element of how someone chooses an action is thus a choice set containing various actions. In the examples we will offer there will not be more than a handful of simple actions to choose from so the choice sets will all be finite.

To turn to the second question, where do all these actions come from? One answer one may be tempted to give is that they come from the agent himself though another answer that also arises is that they come from the physical and social environment. After all, Phil is capable of walking or taking the bus and so those actions are available to him, but equally, the city provides a pavement and a bus service and so it also plays a role. As a little thought will show, the actions come jointly from both the agent and the environment; neither one by itself suffices to make an action possible. Additionally, an agent's capabilities and an environment's offerings are not enough by themselves: the agent must also be aware of the relevant possibilities. If Phil has just moved into the neighborhood and does not know there is a bus stop nearby, he cannot choose to take the bus.

To those familiar with Gibsonian psychology, it will seem that actions are very similar to affordances and choice sets to what are called ecological niches, that is, collections of affordances. We have just pointed out a key difference: an agent does not need to be aware of his affordances but he does need to know he can act in certain ways in order to make a choice. Another difference is that niches are generally infinite because many irrelevant actions—such as jogging or sprinting to work—are also included in them whereas choice sets typically contain only the relevant actions and so, in the contexts we will consider, are usually quite small. This is because the former notion is constrained primarily by the physical environment and an agent's body whereas the latter is determined by such constraints as well as by higher-order preferences or goals an agent may have such as getting to his place of work in a "reasonable" way. Thus, choice sets for our purposes will just be (very small) subsets of niches with all the extraneous stuff discarded.

Preferences

This brings us to the second element in choice theory, an agent's preferences over his set of actions. Recall that we said earlier that Phil's initial preference was to take the bus and this was expressed by *take the bus* $>$ *walk*.

Once he encountered the street, his preference changed to *walk* $>$ *take the bus*. If the choice set was instead comprised of the three actions *a, b, c*, that is, if $C = \{a, b, c\}$, then there might be all kinds of preferences such as $a > b$ and $b > c$ and so on. As we have tried to show, such preferences are the key to predicting and explaining behavior.

Preferences are relational, that is, they relate a pair of actions. This aspect of preferences can sometimes be cumbersome. There is another equivalent[12] and very familiar way to think about actions that is not relational but also allows comparisons. Everyone has heard of cost-benefit analyses. Each action considered by itself has some benefits and some costs. Phil's walking to work may be assumed to have a benefit of 10 units because it contributes to his health and a cost of 4 units because it takes time and effort and so, overall, he would get a net benefit of $10 - 4 = 6$ units. These numbers are to an extent arbitrary: it is roughly their relative magnitudes that matter. This net benefit is also called utility and there is an elaborate technical account of this concept in economics.[13] For us, all that is required is to compare the net benefits or utilities of different actions. Phil's taking the bus may yield a benefit of only 6 units because there are no particular gains for his health but it gets him to his workplace comfortably and its cost may be 2 units as it takes less time and effort than walking. So its utility is $6 - 2 = 4$ units. The utilities of these two actions may be expressed by utility(*walk*) = benefit(*walk*) − cost(*walk*) = $10 - 4 = 6$ and utility(*take the bus*) = benefit(*take the bus*) − cost(*take the bus*) = $6 - 2 = 4$.[14] That is, utility(*walk*) = 6 and utility(*take the bus*) = 4. Since the utility of walking is 6 and of taking the bus is 4, the former utility or net benefit is higher and so walking is preferred to taking the bus. In other words, *walk* $>$ *take the bus* as we had before. These two ways of thinking about rational actions are parallel to each other and give the same results and sometimes one formulation is more convenient to use and sometimes the other. Experiences and interpretations are better understood in terms of preferences and calculations with benefits and costs help us to more readily see which action is the best for an agent.

It is now possible to answer the question we posed in the previous section. There we said it was merely a claim that:

cheerful street → preference for walking

and also that:

depressing street → preference for taking the bus

but there was no explanation of these crucial facts. How can one explain and even predict that the influences aren't reversed?

It is clear that a cheerful and attractive street offers a significantly greater benefit to Phil's health than a depressing street as he gets the same physical exercise on both kinds of street but the former lifts his mood and the experience is very pleasant. This is self-evident from our human make-up and is probably partly hardwired and partly cultural. If the benefit from a cheerful street is 10 as was said above then it is reasonable to say that the benefit from a depressing street is 5, the difference between the two being attributed to the positive effect of the cheerful street on Phil's mood. The costs of walking remain identical as it takes the same time and effort for Phil to walk to work whether the street is cheerful or depressing.

The utility of the cheerful street is therefore benefit(*cheerful street*) − cost(*cheerful street*) = 10 − 4 = 6 and the utility of the depressing street is benefit(*depressing street*) − cost(*depressing street*) = 5 − 4 = 1. The utility of taking the bus is, as before, benefit(*take the bus*) − cost(*take the bus*) = 6 − 2 = 4. So, in decreasing order, the three utilities are:

$$\begin{aligned}
\text{utility}(\textit{walk on cheerful street}) &= 6 \\
\text{utility}(\textit{take the bus}) &= 4 \\
\text{utility}(\textit{walk on depressing street}) &= 1
\end{aligned}$$

This order can also be equivalently expressed in terms of preferences:

walk on cheerful street > *take the bus* > *walk on depressing street*

Since Phil is rational, he will choose the action that offers the highest utility or net benefit. If he is comparing walking on a cheerful street with taking the bus, he will choose to walk, but if he is comparing walking on a depressing street with taking the bus, he will take the bus!

This is a neat explanation of the earlier claim that:

cheerful street → preference for walking

and also that:

depressing street → preference for taking the bus

Indeed, if it is known in advance what the relative benefits and costs of the three options are, it is possible to predict what Phil will do when he sets out to work, assuming of course that there are no extraneous factors that intrude.

Notice why this really is an explanation of Phil's walking to his office. We did not merely say that the cheerful street was inviting and so he decided to walk. We identified the relative benefits and costs of each of the options—based on reasonable assumptions about our human make-up—and then compared the resulting utilities. In other words, the theory we used did some *work*: it allowed us to break the problem down into its components and introduced a mechanism for comparing actions. It provided a reason why a cheerful street is inviting and a depressing street is not. The other theoretical and practical approaches we have discussed briefly are unable to offer such a detailed analysis of this seemingly simple phenomenon of why a well-designed and attractive street is more appealing.

The analysis in terms of benefits and costs made it easier to appreciate the argument because it was numerical. We could have argued to the same conclusion using qualitative preferences.

But the clever architect will persist: of what practical use is such a theoretical explanation? After all, she already knows intuitively that a cheerful street is inviting. So what does the theory really add to this? The answer is that in some situations it *will* be more or less obvious what Phil will do but in other situations the problem may be more subtle. Let's deepen the analysis by one level.

Suppose what is being compared by Phil (and therefore by the designers) is not a cheerful street versus a depressing street where the outcome may be obvious but a shorter walk versus a longer walk on a cheerful street. Say the shorter walk is 20 minutes and the longer walk is 35 minutes. Then it is not so obvious that the attractiveness of the street will persuade Phil to walk in both cases. It may well be that his benefits and costs for each of the options are such that the utility for the shorter walk is 6 as we had above but for the longer walk it drops to 2 because of its greater cost. Then the utilities could be as follows:

$$\text{utility}(20 \textit{ minute walk on cheerful street}) \quad = \quad 6$$
$$\text{utility}(\textit{take the bus}) \quad = \quad 4$$
$$\text{utility}(35 \textit{ minute walk on cheerful street}) \quad = \quad 2$$
$$\text{utility}(20 \textit{ minute walk on depressing street}) \quad = \quad 1$$
$$\text{utility}(35 \textit{ minute walk on depressing street}) \quad = \quad 0$$

Such utility numbers or preferences can be inferred by a commonsense cost-benefit analysis or obtained through a questionnaire or survey. Only after such a study does it become clear that Phil would opt for the 20-minute walk but he would prefer the bus to a 35-minute walk.

The deeper understanding gained via applying choice theory should convince the skeptical designer that such theoretical insights can make a real contribution to the design process, especially when it is oriented to matters like health. It is in fact seldom obvious what users will do, because many complicating factors are simultaneously present in any real architectural environment and they require detailed and patient analyses. Trade-offs involving many variables are not so easy to grasp intuitively.

Rationality

Keep in mind that what we are exhibiting is how Phil chooses an action to perform from an array of choices available to him. So far we have accounted for the options themselves and how they may be compared. The most obvious question that arises after we have a choice set and utilities or net benefits assigned to the actions is how an agent actually decides what to do. And the answer is equally obvious: he chooses the action with the highest utility or net benefit (or equivalently, he chooses his most preferred option, as explained earlier). This, however, turns out to be a somewhat subtle thing and so it is justified by assuming that the agent in question is *rational*.

The reason it is subtle is that rational agents do not form any odd set of preferences. There are two conditions they must satisfy. These are *transitivity* and *completeness*.

A preference relation on a choice set C is *transitive* if whenever $x \succ y$ and $y \succ z$ then $x \succ z$. Concretely, if Phil prefers avocado to beet and beet to carrot then he is going to also prefer avocado to carrot. This seems quite commonsensical. If he were to prefer carrot to avocado, we would think his preferences were mutually contradictory. Unfortunately, as many behavioral economists have shown through experiments, people often violate transitivity and behave *intransitively*.

A preference relation on a choice set C is *complete* if for all x and y in C either $x > y$ or $y > x$ or $x \sim y$. Recall that the sign $\sim$ means the agent is neutral or indifferent between the two options. Concretely, if Phil can choose between avocado and beet then he always has an explicit comparison between them: either he prefers one to the other or is indifferent between them.[15]

When the choice sets being considered are finite, agents whose preferences conform to completeness and transitivity and who pick their most preferred actions are rational agents. So "rationality" is not just a colloquial term as it is commonly used in ordinary conversation. It is also not a qualitative philosophical or psychological notion. It may be called *economic* rationality as it originated in economics. It consists of the two conditions above and the stipulation that a rational agent selects the most preferred actions. This can be thought of as a *theory* of rationality, one approach to pinning down the concept precisely. As we will show, such precision helps to advance the science of choice in definite, testable ways by allowing us to make sharper distinctions.

This particular account of rationality has been a mainstay of conventional choice theory and its use is widespread in economics, psychology, and other social sciences. It is the standard framework for studying decision-making today though in most uses the theory takes on a more complicated form because of the presence of uncertainty. In our applications here, there will not be any uncertain situations so the form of our theory is relatively simple.

Implicit in this account of rationality is a principle called *invariance*. It is the assumption that when agents are presented with the same choices with no other extraneous factors, they will always form the same preferences. If Phil prefers walking to the bus in the absence of other distractions, he will always prefer it in the same circumstances. Apart from preferences sometimes being incomplete and intransitive, it is this principle that can also be flouted. This occurs most commonly with so-called *framing effects*. When identical choices are framed or presented differently, they can lead to different decisions. Briefly, it is the equivalent of judging a book by its cover, and we will look at examples of such behavior later.

So agents are not always rational in this strict economic sense. When they are not, we will say they are *irrational*. But this term should be understood only as a departure from *economic* rationality. Clearly, labeling various choices as rational and irrational in this way raises many difficult normative issues. There are many situations where what we call rational here will seem like the right thing to observe and a deviation from it will seem right to call irrational. There are as many different kinds of situations where the "irrational" choice will appear quite acceptable and reasonable. There is as yet no consensus about how to deal with these ambiguities. We will stick to this terminology and urge the reader to bear in mind that the reality is messier than Figure 2.3 reveals and that we are using the words in a theoretical rather than intuitive way.

As we had hinted earlier, we will not be able to use utility numbers when actions are not rational as such numbers may not accurately mirror irrational preferences. So we will use utilities when we can and do without them when we cannot.[16] It will be possible to use other types of numbers called *gains* and *losses* and their *values* based on Tversky and Kahneman's prospect theory and we will do so later.

It should be evident by now that matters involving choice can be complicated.

One more such distinction based on adapting an idea of Ariely's is that sometimes we predict we would act in one way but we actually choose differently when faced with the options. We may not violate any of the principles of (economic) rationality in such situations but nevertheless there is a kind of inconsistency between our projections or expectations and our actions. We will call such actions *inconsistent* even though they are still rational.[17] Most actions are consistently rational as they involve straightforwardly predictable behavior.[18] There is just one kind of inconsistently rational behavior we will look at, but we identify the category as it can be useful. Thus, rational actions subdivide into consistent and inconsistent ones as shown in Figure 2.4.

All actions are either consistent, inconsistent, or irrational. It should be remarked that this classification like that of others is meant to be informal. Adopting somewhat different terminology could result in different groupings and we have tailored our definitions to our purposes. All the architectural examples we consider here will be of one of these three types and their analyses will be correspondingly different. We will soon look at a sharply inconsistent choice and then an irrational choice.

Figure 2.3 Classification of human actions at the first level

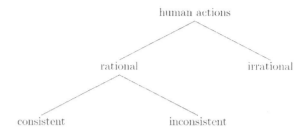

Figure 2.4 Classification of human actions at the second level

In the previous section, we used the pair (choices, preferences) to define the meaning or interpretation of an element of the built environment. Since it is cumbersome to refer to this composite object, we will give it a name. Let's call it *a choice problem C* as that is what Phil and other agents must "solve" to decide what to do. In other words, C(Phil) = (choices, preferences). For Phil, only two options are being compared so the choice problem is simple: C(Phil) = (choices, preferences) = ({*walk, take the bus*}, {*walk* ≻ *take the bus*}). Its solution is for Phil to walk. That is, as a rational agent Phil will choose to walk.

Even when Phil behaves irrationally, he will still face choice problems made up of a choice set and a set of situated or context-based preferences. The only difference will be that the preferences will not be rational and so new principles of choice will apply.

Let's go back to the general schema we outlined:

experience: (choices, preferences) → action

Here the first part (choices, preferences) is just a choice problem and the action that ensues is its solution. It can be re-expressed as:

experience: C → action

In other words, the relevant part of Phil's architectural experience is just his choice problem followed by his optimal choice of walking. This also allows us to see what meanings are in an unusually succinct way:

meaning of street = Phil's choice problem = C(Phil)

And, more abstractly:

meaning of built environment = choice problem = C

This is the essence of our framework for architectural interpretation. The meaning of a street is just the choice problem it induces. Likewise the meaning of various elements of the built environment are also just other choice problems. So we can write either:

built environment → meaning → action → effects on health

as we had before, or equivalently:

built environment → choice problem → action → effects on health

It is interesting that something as seemingly ineffable as architectural interpretation can be addressed by what may appear as mere arithmetic. But used in the right way, numbers and qualitative comparisons can be very powerful tools and can be extended to the most remote corners of human experience. Some people find such theorizing too reductive. They feel it leaves out too much of the nuance, texture, and feel of experience. This can be true and so it is important to always keep the whole situation in mind and go back and forth between it and the abstractions we have described. This guards against common errors that arise when the restricted contexts in which the framework is constructed are forgotten and the theory is applied indiscriminately.

2.5 Extending this Model to the Community

In developing this model of architectural experience and interpretation, we have pointed out that in order to predict the solution to Phil's choice problem accurately it is necessary to assume that no extraneous factors intervene, that other things are equal. In reality, however, there may be all kinds of unwanted influences: he could be late for work, he may have plans to go to the gym later in the day, Tom may offer him a ride, and so on. In other words, the choice problem induced by Phil's surrounding built environment may change from day to day and so its solution, the action he undertakes, also changes daily. We need to look at Phil's behavior over a longer time period, say a year, and see if designing a salubrious street experience increases the number of times he chooses to walk.

Moreover, the architect is not designing exclusively for Phil, important though he may be for us. We are interested in improving the health of the whole community. Tom and others in the neighborhood may have quite different circumstances. What has to be targeted is an overall increase in walking across the relevant population. A few representative choice problems with somewhat different choice sets and preferences over them have to be studied. This requires looking at a collection of choice problems and computing "average" solutions: how much more will people walk over the year, and so on. Then such percentage increases or decreases have to be measured empirically to see if the theoretical predictions are borne out.

Changing choice problems across time and space are not the only source of variation in whether a community takes to walking more often than not. As we have been discussing, many economists and psychologists have recently found systematic ways in which human beings deviate from this kind of economic rationality. In a recent popular book *Thinking, Fast and Slow*, Kahneman has argued that we think in two ways that he dubs "fast" and "slow" and the fast way sometimes leads us to errors that we would not commit if we were to deliberate more slowly and carefully.[19] This book and similar ones provide examples that are rich and diverse, and it is this intuitive form of the theory that offers the most compelling way to understand architecture.

2.6 The Architectural Problem

We have described Phil's and his neighbors' architectural encounters as choice problems. We have also said that architecture is a two-sided communicative process. It is now time to look at the architectural problem more closely.

As designers, architects must clarify the functions they want to support. If health is one of them, as it increasingly is today in many parts of the world, they will need some theoretical understanding of the connection between architecture and health. If they decide to use the framework we are offering, they would start by anticipating the choice problems that are likely to arise in the relevant community. Indeed, differently put, the architectural problem is precisely to *design* choice problems for users. That is, they must offer the kinds of choices that induce healthy actions among a statistically significant proportion of the population over an extended period of time. In their popular book *Nudge*, Thaler and Sunstein call such designers of choice problems in a policy context *choice architects*.[20] Our kind of architect is therefore a choice architect in a double sense: she is an architect and she has to design choices as well.

So far we have been looking at a fairly simple kind of choice situation. In practice, there will be many choice problems that exist simultaneously in any given environment not only because there are multiple users with different circumstances and profiles but also because something like a street has multiple uses and there are multiple elements like streets in any real architectural problem.

To implement this model, an architectural team would have to carry out a comprehensive and detailed *mapping* as it were of the whole situation all the way down to benefits and costs and resulting utilities where they might apply or to preferences, or Tversky and Kahneman's values where they might not. They have to be mindful of the fact that utilities, values, and preferences are rough and approximate and that they have to be estimated loosely. For this, surveys and questionnaires may be required or just intuitive analyses as we said before. Once this is done teams have to relate the architectural means at their disposal to these choice problems.

Actually, the process is not quite sequential as we have just described it. It is a back-and-forth one involving some initial means and architectural ideas that lead to a mapping of choice problems and the solutions to these reflect back on the means and devices available to architects, often triggering new demands and new ideas if the earlier ones were inadequate. It is a complex holistic process that is familiar to architects but with some new elements mixed in involving choice theory and a new conception of the meanings the built environment holds for users.

In a sense the architectural problem, considered even beyond the narrower confines of health in its full generality, is also a choice problem because the architect has many ways to realize her ambitions and fulfill the program. Some of these choices may be readily evident, others may emerge through a creative process in a more or less unexpected manner. So it is difficult to specify a choice set for her as it is only partially formed and evolving. Besides, in an entire project there will be many levels and types of choices (e.g. a whole residential building, the layout of individual floors, and the plan for each apartment) and so it may not be useful to view her problem as a choice problem except in a loose, metaphorical way. On the other hand, the architectural process is becoming increasingly automated and it is quite possible that choice theory could have a role to play in an algorithmic process that provides support to an architect's team. That is, there could conceivably be a double use of choice theory, one to better understand how users will respond to the alternative designs and the other to model the architectural process itself.

2.7 Phil Can Sometimes be Inconsistently Rational

We said earlier that trade-offs involving multiple variables can be hard to intuit. Not only is this difficult for architects, it is also difficult for Phil.

Building on an example from Ariely's *Predictably Irrational*,[21] suppose Phil frequents a neighborhood eatery where he generally chooses one of two items on the menu, the first priced $9 and the second $13. This is his choice set, a subset of the larger number of offerings on the menu. Maybe the first is a soup and the second a salad. They are a bit hard to compare as they provide somewhat different gustatory pleasures. So he tends to unconsciously go for the less expensive soup taking the benefits of both to be more or less equal. If the salad is a and the soup b then $b > a$ much of the time. He does order the salad occasionally to vary what he eats but he predominantly has the soup.

Phil's choice problem in this new environment is thus C(Phil) = (choices, preferences) = ($\{a, b\}, \{b > a\}$). That is, C(Phil) is the meaning the menu holds for him. This allows us to say as we did before in the case of the street:

restaurant menu $\rightarrow$ meaning $\rightarrow$ soup $\rightarrow$ gustatory and other effects

It is helpful to see this formulation of a very different situation using the same framework because it reveals how general it is. In the same way, it will also apply to all kinds of architectural settings.

The restaurateur now introduces a new salad c that is the most expensive appetizer at \$15. Very few customers, including Phil, order c because it is the costliest among their choices even though it appears desirable. Now Phil finds himself shifting from the soup b to the second most expensive item on his list, the less costly salad a. So do many of the other customers.

It may even happen that he now orders a much more than he did b in the earlier scenario. If he used to have the soup about 70% of the time he may now be eating the cheaper of the two salads about 80% of the time. Not only does Phil's initial preference reverse itself, he even gravitates proportionally more to a.

This is completely unexpected and even astonishing behavior because adding the new item c ought not to change the relative benefits and costs of a and b but it does, given the way most of us act. Why does it happen? As Ariely says, people seldom see things in absolute terms. They tend to focus on the relative advantage of one thing over another. Not only this, when two things are difficult to compare—like an apple and an orange or a soup and a salad—they avoid such comparisons and shift to relatively easier ones such as a red apple and a green apple or two different salads. Ariely calls this principle *relativity* because it works by first recognizing that certain things—like culinary preparations—are difficult to compare and then by noticing what people generally do when faced with various prices or costs.

Let's take a closer look at Phil's behavior. There are two related but different reasons for the change in his preferences.

One is that the less expensive salad now seems more accessible as there is a more expensive salad. This also makes it relatively more desirable. Correspondingly, the soup's being the cheapest item gets magnified in his perception and this makes it relatively *un*desirable.

A second reason is that the soup and salad are harder to compare than the two salads and the less expensive salad appears better overall than the new more expensive salad. As *a* looks like a better choice than *c* it also seems better than *b* even though the two are difficult to compare one on one.

Initially Phil's general preference was *b* > *a*; now, for these two reasons, his general preference switches to *a* > *b* > *c*. The new item *c* is almost never selected itself but it has influenced Phil to shift from *b* to *a*. So *c* acts like a magnet, pulling Phil and other customers upward. Such a design does not work in absolute terms but statistically across most customers and over an extended period.

The new meaning of the menu is *C*(Phil) = (choices, preferences) = ({*a, b, c*}, {*a* > *b, b* > *c, a* > *c*}). The set of preferences contains more than one preference in this more complicated situation. Another way of describing what happens after *c* is added to the menu is that its meaning changes for Phil and other customers. As we have seen, this new choice problem leads to a different action:

> restaurant menu → new meaning → cheaper salad → different gustatory
> and other effects

If this change in Phil's behavior were pointed out to him, he would himself be surprised. He would not have predicted that he would act this way when he was perfectly happy ordering the soup. His behavior is *inconsistent* by our definition of the term because there is a discrepancy between his expected and actual behavior. He is still perfectly rational because he has not contravened any of its conditions including the implicit principle of invariance. The two choice sets are different: first it was {*a, b*} and later it became {*a, b, c*} and invariance requires that the behavior in identical choice situations be the same. So Phil is inconsistently rational if only by a hair's breadth. That is, he is spared from being called irrational just because of a technicality in the way invariance is defined.

The statistical switch from *b* to *a* can also be explained by assigning utilities to the various options. The key point is that the reversal of Phil's preferences is accompanied by a corresponding reversal of his utilities. Concretely, maybe benefit(*a*) = benefit(*b*) = 20 earlier, and cost(*a*) = 13 and cost(*b*) = 9 as we might expect from their prices,[22] and so utility(*a*) = 20 − 13 = 7 and utility(*b*) = 20 − 9 = 11. This means *b* > *a* as we presented above.

When the new salad *c* is introduced, the benefit of the old, cheaper salad *a* jumps to 25 as it now appears more accessible and relatively more desirable. This also happens because the relative benefit of *a* gets crystallized by comparison with *c*. As a result, *a*'s new utility is 25 − 13 = 12 and *b*'s utility is $20 - 9 = 11$ as before. The utility of c is generally the lowest of the three, say $24 - 15 = 9$. Earlier we had:

utility(b) = 11
utility(a) = 7

These utilities now become:

utility(a) = 12
utility(b) = 11
utility(c) = 9

These calculations explain in more detail how the reversal in preferences emerges. It is not that Phil actually evaluates these costs and benefits consciously. They just occur in a rapid unconscious blur—"fast thinking" as Kahneman puts it—and Phil is to be viewed only as if he was computing utilities. The utility analysis mirrors or correlates with his inner comparisons that neuroscience is only now beginning to understand. Sometimes, though, when Phil feels somewhat indecisive he may deliberate more self-consciously.

There are many such situations in everyday life. The question for us is whether architects and the city can do Phil a service by making use of this principle of relativity in the built environment. The idea is to nudge him and

Figure 2.5 A not so cheerful but also not so depressing street

his neighborhood toward healthier choices overall. Can a suitable architectural magnet be found?

Imagine a slightly different scenario where Phil's cheerful street is now not quite so dazzling but is nevertheless not depressing. It becomes harder for him to compare its attractions with his other option of taking the bus which does offer a comfortable ride. Considering that walking takes more time and effort, he may divide his choices evenly between the two or may even prefer the bus. If walking is a and taking the bus is b then we may generally have $b > a$ just as we had with the soup and salad at the beginning. Indeed, the meaning of the street appears identical to the meaning of the menu when expressed in symbols:

$$\text{meaning of street} = C(\text{Phil}) = (\text{choices, preferences}) = (\{a, b\}, \{b > a\})$$

The symbols a and b represent different things in the case of the restaurant and the case of the street but their structure is the same. This helps us to see the analogy we are constructing because there is an exact correspondence between the two situations. The resulting action in the architectural situation is:

$$\text{street} \rightarrow \text{meaning} \rightarrow \textit{take the bus} \rightarrow \text{poor effects on health}$$

Just because when considered abstractly the two situations are the same, this does not mean that everything in one will automatically carry over to the other. However, it is plausible to expect that some things will.

Figure 2.6 A not so cheerful but also not so depressing street with a bike lane

We would like Phil to choose walking more often. There are multiple ways this might be attempted. Suppose the architect creates a brightly demarcated bike lane on the street. This is option *c*, an architectural analogue of the new expensive salad. Offering biking is similar to offering the new salad in some but not all ways. Where it is different is that there may be a larger group, relatively speaking, of biking enthusiasts who take up biking. That is, not many customers opt for the expensive salad but relatively more of Phil's neighbors do take up biking. Phil himself, however, while he feels the attraction of the vigorous exercise and healthier living it promises, prefers a lower level of activity, especially on his way to work. In this new context, Phil shifts to the second most desirable choice, walking. Earlier he used to take the bus more often than not; now he might walk even more, proportionately speaking. This effect is similar to Phil's switching from the soup to the cheaper salad. The architectural analogue of biking has some consequences that are similar and some that are not.

Phil's kind of behavior, if it really does occur, would be equally unexpected and equally astonishing. The prediction is that not only do relatively more people bike (than opt for the expensive salad) but also that even more people shift from taking the bus to walking. Such a hypothesis would have to be tested empirically of course. Introducing a bike lane carries a double benefit potentially: it *directly* enables biking but *indirectly* encourages more walking. The direct benefit is easy to see and to predict. The sort of insight required for the indirect benefit is available only through a theoretical approach. When a city decides to provide bike lanes, it typically does this only for the direct benefit of "natural" bikers. It is the principle of relativity applied to this new domain that enables us to anticipate the indirect benefit.

How would we explain Phil's switch to walking?

First, recall that the new expensive salad is seen as the most desirable partly on account of its price but is also relatively inaccessible for that very reason because in general it is human nature not to go for the most expensive item. And it is equally human nature not to select the cheapest item out of a list of three or more. In the same way, Phil feels the attraction of biking because he associates it with healthy living. But he is not oriented to this level of activity: it is too costly precisely because of the much greater effort involved and also because he would have to get hold of a bike, take it to work, park it somewhere, and so on. In his mind, biking gets ranked as the most desirable choice but one that is not for him owing to its higher costs. But this very desirability nudges him "upward" to walking as now taking the bus appears relatively undesirable.

Second, just as the soup and salad are somewhat difficult to compare, so are walking and taking the bus. Just as the two salads are easier to compare and the cheaper salad appears better *overall*, so also walking and biking are easier to compare as both involve exercise and health, and walking is preferred *overall*. This will make it seem like a better option than taking the bus as well, as Phil now has two healthy alternatives.

So his general preferences will switch from $b > a$ to $a > b > c$ or *walk > take the bus > bike*. The new meaning of the street now is:

new meaning of street = C(Phil) = (choices, preferences) = ($\{a, b, c\}$, $\{a > b, b > c, a > c\}$)

This is identical in structure to the new meaning of the restaurant menu so we can see that the analogy is exact. And in this architectural situation, it leads to a healthier action overall for Phil.

street $\rightarrow$ new meaning $\rightarrow$ *walk* $\rightarrow$ better effects on health

For the same reasons as before, Phil is inconsistently rational in this new architectural setting where he is influenced to adopt a healthier choice. Phil is likely to be equally surprised at this change in his behavior—at how a new bike path gets him to walk more often. A parallel set of utility-based rankings could once again be applied but the idea should now be clear so we will not belabor the point.

2.8 How Tom's Irrationality Can Sometimes Help Him

Irrationality is just as relevant as inconsistency in our actions.

Tom, Phil's neighbor, currently earns \$135,000 and has a daily commute of 20 minutes. He is now being offered a new job at a different salary and with a different travel time. The new salary is higher by \$10,000 but he would have to spend an extra hour commuting. So while he would gain in one dimension he would lose in another. Assume the magnitude of the relative gain from the new salary is roughly the same for Tom as the magnitude of the relative loss from the new commute. So Tom decides to pass up the offer because it would cut into the time he can spend with his family. If the raise had been \$20,000, he reasons, he may have considered it. Alternatively, if the additional travel time had been 20 minutes, he could have

accommodated it. As things stand, the trade-off isn't worth it. This situation can be expressed succinctly as follows:

Existing job: (\$135,000 salary, 20 minute travel time) $= (s_1, t_1)$
New job: (\$145,000 salary, 80 minute travel time) $= (s_2, t_2)$

In this choice situation, Tom has the preference $(s_1, t_1) \succ (s_2, t_2)$. That is, he prefers his current job.

Now we consider a hypothetical situation where the facts above are exactly reversed. Tom's existing job is (s_2, t_2), the new one he was offered previously and refused, and he is now being offered (s_1, t_1), his earlier job. In other words:

Existing job: (\$145,000 salary, 80 minute travel time) $= (s_2, t_2)$
New job: (\$135,000 salary, 20 minute travel time) $= (s_1, t_1)$

One would expect that because earlier Tom's preference was $(s_1, t_1) \succ (s_2, t_2)$, he would change jobs this time because his choices would be as before: he has to choose between (s_1, t_1) and (s_2, t_2) again. This is what rational choice theory would predict by the principle of invariance. But amazingly, Tom now finds himself thinking of the advantages of his current situation—the twice-weekly restaurant outing he would have to reduce to once a week and sundry other items he would have to give up. The shorter commute doesn't seem so important because he's been doing the longer commute for several years and is now used to it, using the time to catch up on his reading. If the cut in pay had been \$5,000 instead of \$10,000, he reasons this time, he might have accepted it. So now he has the opposite preference $(s_2, t_2) \succ (s_1, t_1)$ and passes up the offer again. In other words, he disobeys the principle of invariance, making different decisions in identical choice situations, and as a result he is irrational by definition.

When we are given similar choices in real life, we invariably prefer the status quo as Tom does. This has been extensively tested empirically in diverse scenarios where there is a choice between the status quo and some alternative that is advantageous in some respects and disadvantageous in others and the magnitudes of these advantages and disadvantages are roughly the same.[23] It is a little bit like saying the grass is greener on this side when we are faced with an actual choice of this kind.

Why does this happen? The only difference in the two situations is Tom's current context in each setting. So it must be playing some role. In the first scenario, the loss of family time seemed to be the decisive factor. In the second scenario, the loss of extra cash seemed pivotal. In both cases, the

losses outweighed the gains even though their magnitudes were identical. But rational choice theory has no concepts or mechanisms corresponding to context and to losses somehow prevailing over equal gains, and so is unable to explain this behavior.

Recall that when Phil weighed his benefits and costs, he didn't need to consider his current situation. The costs and benefits didn't exert disproportionate influences. In his circumstances, it was fine to evaluate his options as he did. Now Tom's seemingly contradictory behavior forces us to look for new ideas that can resolve this paradox. Kahneman and Tversky's prospect theory offers precisely what we need. With just a few modifications of utility theory, it shows how when the relevant gains and losses are roughly equal relative to a context, the losses will appear larger than the gains and so people will generally prefer the status quo.

Prospect theory's first interesting insight is that people measure gains and losses from a reference point, the technical term for a context. In Tom's first choice situation, this reference point is just the existing job (s_1, t_1). In his second hypothetical choice situation, the reference point is the hypothetical existing job (s_2, t_2).

First situation: Reference point = (s_1, t_1)
Second situation: Reference point = (s_2, t_2)

Such reference points or contexts are always present in our decisions. They are perhaps the key missing element in utility theory. No mention was made of Phil's reference dependence because in his situation it didn't make any difference—unless of course some extraneous factor like his being late were to enter the reckoning. But in a number of commonly occurring situations like Tom's, the reference situation makes all the difference.

When Tom evaluates the new job offer in each situation, he tries to see how his current context would change rather than considering the two options abstractly. His approach is to weigh the incremental pluses and minuses rather than the absolute amounts. That is, he does not compare (s_1, t_1) with (s_2, t_2), the two absolute options before him, but assesses the relative differences between the two as seen from different reference points. This is a crucial part of the new story but it isn't enough by itself. Based on his initial reference points in each case, prospect theory further posits that Tom's respective gains and losses from these points have numerical *values*, which are just like numerical utilities but have slightly different attributes. That is, value is a *function* of positive gains and negative losses and this function generally has the S shape shown in Figure 2.7.

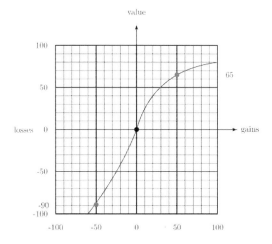

Figure 2.7 The value function: the *S* curve

The figure shows gains from 0 to 100 and losses from 0 to −100 on the X-axis. The $10,000 raise offered to Tom in the first scenario would be a gain and the 60 minute increase in travel time would be a loss. As we have said they are roughly equal in magnitude, the gain could be represented as +50 and the loss could be represented as −50. These increments and decrements are measured from the reference point which is 0 and is shown as a large dot at the origin of the graph. It represents his existing job (s_1, t_1) with its salary of $135,000 and travel time of 20 minutes. Its *value* is 0 because it is the status quo.

The value of gains as represented on the Y-axis is positive and flattens out, a shape that is called concave. In other words, higher and higher salary increments carry diminishing value. We can see from the graph that the value of a gain of +50 in salary is 65 and it is shown by a large dot at (50, 65) in the first quadrant. The value of losses is negative and convex and so shows diminishing sensitivity to larger and larger losses. Again, the value of a loss of −50 from the increased travel time is −90 and it is shown by a large dot at (−50, −90) in the third quadrant.

This leads to prospect theory's second remarkable insight: the value curve is *steeper* on the negative or loss side than the positive or gain side. As we have seen, the value of a *loss* of 50 is −90 and is much greater in magnitude than the value of a *gain* of 50 which is just 65. This property of the value function is called *loss aversion*. It expresses the fact that a loss of a certain size looms larger (in value) than a gain of the same size. The new job offer carries a positive value of 65 and a negative value of −90. This points to the following calculations:

$$\text{value}(s_1, t_1) = 0$$
$$\text{value}(s_2, t_2) = 65 + (-90) = -25$$

As the value of the status quo is higher because of loss aversion, it is preferred and Tom does not change his job. This is so even when the gains and losses are just roughly equal in magnitude: if the loss had been just 40, its value would have been −75, and the value of the whole package would have been value $(s_2, t_2) = 65 + (-75) = -10$, still less than 0.

Now consider the calculations based on Tom's second situation. His reference shifts to (s_2, t_2) with a salary of \$145,000 and a travel time of 80 minutes. He now measures the new job offer from this vantage point. Its value is now 0. From (s_2, t_2), the new salary s_1 drops by \$10,000 and leads to a loss of −50 and the new commute t_1 is shorter by 60 minutes and leads to a gain of +50. What happens to Tom in this situation is that the shift in his reference turns previous gains into losses and vice versa and this leads to a reversal in his preference from $(s_1, t_1) > (s_2, t_2)$ to $(s_2, t_2) > (s_1, t_1)$.

$$\text{value}(s_2, t_2) = 0$$
$$\text{value}(s_1, t_1) = (-90) + 65 = -25$$

In each situation, therefore, the new job offer appears worse. This explains and even predicts Tom's surprising behavior. We made use of two important ideas, reference dependence and loss aversion. Utility theory does not have either. So we have to use prospect theory to explain such irrational behavior.

We can now apply these insights to our architectural domain. Recall that Tom sometimes walks to work and sometimes drives. Assume he is back to just the attractive street without the bike lane. Suppose that he walks 40% of the time and drives 60% of the time. Let his proportion of walking be represented by s_1 and his proportion of driving by t_1.[24] Then his reference point will be what characterizes his existing situation, namely $(s_1, t_1) = (40\%, 60\%)$. Earlier (s_1, t_1) represented the two dimensions of his existing job, his salary and his travel time, now the same symbols represent the two dimensions of his getting to work, the proportion of time he walks and the proportion of time he drives.

As the neighborhood grows, so does the traffic congestion. The city contemplates widening the road by narrowing the pavements. This would make driving easier and so is a gain for Tom. But it would also make walking worse and so is a loss for him. Under these conditions, he would walk only 20% of the time and drive 80% of the time. We can represent this new proposal by $(s_2, t_2) = (20\%, 80\%)$. The drop in the proportion of walking from 40% to 20% is a loss as measured from his reference point (s_1, t_1). We can represent this as a loss of -50 as before. Likewise the driving becomes pleasanter and so represents a gain of $+50$ from (s_1, t_1).

It should be evident that this architectural situation is exactly analogous to Tom's earlier job situation. There is both an advantage and a disadvantage to the new proposal of expanding the road. Keep in mind that he does not compare the absolute option (s_1, t_1), the wider pavement and narrower road, with the other absolute option (s_2, t_2), the narrower pavement and wider road, but only the relative gains and losses. This suggests that Tom will again prefer the status quo where he is walking more and driving less. In our arithmetical language, value(s_1, t_1) > value(s_2, t_2) by the same calculations as before.

In this case, the irrationality arising from his loss aversion helps him and he chooses the healthier option of the wider pavement and narrower road as it will enable him to maintain his current higher proportion of walking $s_1 = 40\%$ which would drop to $s_2 = 20\%$ if the pavement became more constricted.

Incredibly, if the situation had been exactly reversed, if the wider road and narrower pavement had been the reference, and if the city were proposing to widen the pavement by narrowing the road to encourage

Figure 2.8 A cheerful street with a wider road and narrower pavement

walking, or if it were planning a healthier bike lane option, he would nevertheless prefer the new status quo because this time value$(s_2, t_2) >$ value(s_1, t_1) as the former gains turn into losses and vice versa. This time the irrationality leads to an unhealthier choice of $(s_2, t_2) = (20\%, 80\%)$ over $(s_1, t_1) = (40\%, 60\%)$, but now we have an explanation of this behavior—reference dependence and loss aversion—and are even able to predict it.

In terms of our framework of interpretation, the meaning of the architectural situation isn't stable and always depends on the reference point in addition to the choices it affords. Such examples show how subtle the problem of designing architectural choices for a community can be, very different from obvious initiatives like providing adequate lighting to make spaces safe, as we said in our opening paragraphs.

Going back to the first situation where the congestion has built up on the narrower road, if the city were aware of such irrationalities, it could opt to adjust the duration of the traffic signals in order to reduce the congestion instead of widening the road, a less costly intervention that would also meet with approval from residents like Tom as it would represent a pure gain without any loss and would have a higher value than the status quo.

We introduced a few key ideas of prospect theory to account for Tom's behavior. We could have also used it earlier as it is a more general theory than utility theory and subsumes it, but we wanted to present utility theory as well, and this way the special strengths of prospect theory come to light.

2.9 The Architectural Problem Revisited

The foregoing suggests that an architect needs to think carefully about the choice situation or meaning she will be creating and whether the response to it will be consistent, inconsistent, or irrational. The choice theory we have presented more or less seamlessly accommodates these different behaviors by selecting either utility theory or prospect theory as the appropriate analytic lens through which to view human behavior.

It may seem that the alternative streetscapes we have discussed present architecture itself in the barest of ways. But there are many levels of detail that need to be designed even for a street: the planting of trees and many other decorative elements that distinguish a pleasant street experience from an unpleasant one. Such items will be multiplied manifold as we consider more examples. We have already noted the built environment surrounds us all the time and each of its details is a matter of conscious design.

Not only is it omnipresent, we have also portrayed it as dynamic rather than static, as nudging us to choose one way rather than another. Not only is it not just *frozen* music as Goethe thought, it actively mediates the relationship between the maker and the user as a multisensory *utterance* and experience. Even phenomenology depicts our architectural encounters as relatively passive. The choice set is not just something the person contributes; it is jointly constructed by both the design and the engagement with it. This relational, interactive meaning is partly embedded within architecture itself. It is what moves us to act.

Choice architects' teams will then *model* architectural initiatives as social ventures and anticipate how various communities will react. Many projects not necessarily related to health fail for this very reason: a poor understanding of their meanings for the populations they intend to serve. In a situation where the explicit goal is to nudge people to healthy action this becomes even more compelling.

In this sense, architecture is not just an aesthetic enterprise, it is equally a *social* undertaking, and architects must bring to it the keen insight into social action and society possessed by the social theorist. This makes it very different from the other arts where the goals are exclusively aesthetic. Many architects may feel the social dimension is merely utilitarian and not intellectual, but if seen in a broader way, utility is the most intellectual of objects with deep theoretical underpinnings. Not only that, utility and aesthetics are no longer clearly separate concerns because they interact in all sorts of unexpected ways.

It is partly to emphasize these intellectual foundations that we have related the choice problems architecture engenders to its *meanings*. This is a novel perspective in our view, one that demands a closer, more imbricated or overlapping connection between the Vitruvian realms of utility, firmness, and beauty than has hitherto been acknowledged.

Notes

1 Spiegelberg (1981), Casey (2009).
2 Gibson (1979), Michaels and Carello (1981).
3 Techau et al. (2016).
4 Rush (2009), Shirazi (2014).
5 Zaitchik (2013). See also Maier et al. (2009).
6 Allais (1953), Simon (1955, 1956), Kahneman and Tversky (1979, 1982, 2000), Tversky and Kahneman (2000).
7 Ariely (2008), Thaler and Sunstein (2008), Kahneman (2011).
8 Parikh (2011).
9 Schmidt (2012), Helsing Almass (2013).
10 Notice, though, that when the physical context does change—as it did when the architect I. M. Pei added the glass pyramid to the Louvre—the meaning of the original building also changes.
11 The way to read an expression like "choices(Phil)" is as "choices of Phil." In general, function(x) is read "function of x."

12 This is true only when agents are rational as we discuss below.
13 Utility can be separated into benefits and costs that are then added up only under certain technical conditions.
14 Again, "utility(*walk*)" is read as "utility of *walk*" and so on.
15 The first condition of transitivity must actually be expressed in terms of both preference and indifference but we will ignore this nicety.
16 Indeed, it is because of this possibility that the economic notion of rationality seems to capture something important.
17 Inconsistency can also be irrational of course and that is how Ariely's notion seems to work. That is why we are adapting his notion to our uses and restricting it to rational actions.
18 The criterion that distinguishes consistent from inconsistent actions is relatively informal.
19 Kahneman (2011).
20 Thaler and Sunstein (2008, p. 3).
21 Ariely (2008, pp. 7–10).
22 There is no reason why costs should be assigned the same numerical value as the corresponding prices. Costs are relative numbers whereas prices are absolute numbers. But we have done this to make the arithmetic smoother.
23 Kahneman and Tversky (2000, pp. 13–14).
24 We are deliberately reusing the symbols s and t to see clearly how Tom's response to the built environment is analogous to the earlier situation with his job offer.

3 Rational and Irrational Behavior

In the majority of decisions people make, they are consistently rational. Surprisingly often, though, they are irrational as well.

Most choices we face are analogous to Phil's of walking or taking the bus given that the street is cheerful or not. The architectural setting has a meaning and we simply select the best option based on completeness, transitivity, and invariance although it may occasionally require some ingenuity to correctly assign costs and benefits to different actions. As consistency is relatively straightforward to analyze via a utility analysis or even just by inspecting qualitative preferences, we will look at just one more situation exemplifying it since the situation involves a very different aspect of the built environment and a very different aspect of our health.

As we explained earlier, inconsistent rationality is an unusual category where it is the technical definition of rationality involving the implicit need for invariance that makes certain behaviors unexpected but still rational. We introduced the principle of relativity because it often occurs even in architectural settings. There are not many other such principles that are inconsistent-but-rational and so we will not address this category further.

We will devote the bulk of this chapter to exploring several different ways in which people can be irrational. We will discuss them from architectural vantage points partly by constructing analogies with similar situations in other domains as we did in the previous chapter. As we said before, an interesting feature of our investigation is that we show how irrationality can be turned to one's advantage. It should be borne in mind, however, that our claims are hypotheses. They need to be thoroughly tested through experiments before their predictions can be taken as reliable.

3.1 Back to Consistent Rationality

One day at a meeting where the uninspired performance and diminishing productivity of many people in his workplace are discussed, Phil is tasked with identifying the reasons for this pervasive lack of enthusiasm and engagement. So he discusses the matter with a number of his colleagues, eliciting different sorts of possible causes—none of which seem entirely convincing and call at best for minor improvements. Then Martha, who sits in the office next to his, mentions the unstimulating physical environment itself and how it seems to sap her energy. This resonates with Phil on account of his own experience: he is stuck in an interior office with no windows while the higher-ups have nice large offices along the perimeter of the floor. Working in such a closed environment leaves him dull and dispirited by the end of his day despite his brisk morning walk to the building where his firm has leased a couple of floors. Until now, he had been only dimly aware of the probable source of his lassitude, but now this strikes him with the force of a revelation.

By sheer chance his college alumni association has organized a talk by a well-known local architect. During the cocktail reception, he brings up this question with her casually and she suggests that it is often primarily the lack of natural light in many public and private spaces that creates stressful environments because natural light regulates human circadian rhythms and can dramatically improve a person's mood and efficiency. He realizes immediately how true this is, especially for his windowless room. He also feels there are many trade-offs involved in a workplace that make his situation less than clearcut. So, as a first rational step, he decides to do a cost-benefit analysis of his physical environment as it relates to him. We'll call this environment A for short.

For the benefits of working in A he assigns a score of 4 for the quiet his closed office provides and a score of 3 for privacy. These two benefits are related but distinct as both contribute in somewhat different ways to his concentration, conversations, and output. They yield a total benefit of 4 + 3 = 7. Similarly, he feels a cost of 5 would be appropriate for the lack of sunlight—his most serious complaint—and a cost of 4 for being cut off from his co-workers. These two costs add up to a total cost of 5 + 4 = 9. He then combines these numbers as follows:

$$\begin{aligned} \text{utility}(\textit{work in A}) \ &= \ \text{total benefit}(\textit{work in A}) \ - \ \text{total cost}(\textit{work in A}) \\ &= \ (4+3) - (5+4) \\ &= \ 7 - 9 \\ &= \ -2 \end{aligned}$$

It is logically acceptable for Phil to compute this utility through all these steps as there is no way to guess his overall satisfaction intuitively, but without something to compare it against, it is a *meaningless* exercise in

Figure 3.1 Office environment A

almost a literal sense. There has to be another action as a possible choice that might be called "work in environment B." So he asks an architect friend to do a couple of rough sketches of alternative office layouts that give everyone some access to natural light and social interaction without sacrificing the existing benefits altogether. She advises him that an open office plan with a few closed rooms for meetings might be a better arrangement in his circumstances.

The two plans she creates provide access to natural light through windows to virtually all the occupants either directly or indirectly. They also afford greater visibility across the floor that would allow people to see each other walking about which could lead to increased social interaction. But even the mere sight of co-workers over the course of an entire day can be significant. The conference rooms meant for internal meetings are moved to the interior as no one is likely to spend all of their time there. A couple of meeting rooms for visitors retain impressive views. In one option—call it B—glass-enclosed offices preserve the quiet and privacy the current design makes possible. In the other—call it C—the higher-ups keep many of the privileges they currently enjoy but at some small cost of slightly reduced room sizes.

Phil now has these two alternative actions *work in B* and *work in C* to compare with working in A. As before, he first decides to carry out a personal cost-benefit analysis of the whole choice situation even though B and C are not as yet real options.

In B he would have a glass-enclosed office in the interior with access to *indirect* natural light so he assigns a score of 4 for this new feature, a score of 4 as before for the continued quiet he would enjoy, and a score of

Figure 3.2 Office environment B

1 for the reduced feeling of privacy. The greater social interaction B makes possible garners 5 units. He is pleased to discover there are no real costs except for the slight reduction in privacy owing to the glass enclosure. He combines these new numbers as follows:

$$
\begin{aligned}
\text{utility}(work\ in\ B) &= \text{total benefit}(work\ in\ B) - \text{total cost}(work\ in\ B) \\
&= (4 + 4 + 1 + 5) - 0 \\
&= 14
\end{aligned}
$$

In C he would have an open workstation, even less privacy, and a certain amount of noise from neighbors. His access to natural light would be direct as he would be seated close to a window and his social interaction would also be more intense which could sometimes be a plus and sometimes a minus. So he assigns benefits of 6 for natural light and 4 for social interaction, and costs of 3 for the increased noise level and 1 for the loss of privacy. There is also a bonus benefit of a more uniform and controlled thermal environment, a factor he was unaware of earlier, that he thinks should get a score of 2. This leads to:

$$
\begin{aligned}
\text{utility}(work\ in\ C) &= \text{total benefit}(work\ in\ C) - \text{total cost}(work\ in\ C) \\
&= (6 + 4 + 2) - (3 + 1) \\
&= 12 - 4 \\
&= 8
\end{aligned}
$$

Figure 3.3 Office environment C

He is now able to weigh these options against one another as follows:

utility(*work in A*) = −2
utility(*work in B*) = 14
utility(*work in C*) = 8

The ranking this implies can also be equivalently expressed in terms of preferences:

work in B > *work in C* > *work in A*

In other words, both new designs offer significantly healthier options than his existing situation. Now that there are three options and preferences ordering them, he has a proper choice problem as opposed to his earlier situation when there was just the single option A. He is able to say as he did before when he chose to walk to work rather than take the bus that this expanded choice problem is the *meaning* his workplace acquires. This can be expressed as follows:

meaning of workplace = C(Phil) = (choices, preferences) = ({A, B, C}, {$B > C, C > A, B > A$}))

He realizes, however, that different co-workers could register different costs and benefits and, therefore, different preferences overall and different meanings because they experience somewhat different aspects of their environment. In particular, though people like him would be likely to share similar preferences, the senior employees may feel they are better off with A as their current offices line the perimeter of the floor.

Phil discusses his approach and his initial findings with one of his senior colleagues Naomi. She carries out the same analysis from her own point of view. She currently has a large corner office with lots of sunshine, quiet, and privacy but also misses the social access and uniform thermal atmosphere that Phil has identified. Option B would result in her office becoming smaller and various benefits reducing proportionately, whereas option C trades off social visibility and interaction and also a better thermal environment with a slightly reduced office size. Additionally, her office would be enclosed by glass in B and C to permit natural light to reach the interior so she would have somewhat reduced privacy in both. Without going into the details of her cost-benefit calculations, her overall utilities turn out to be:

utility(*work in A*) = 6
utility(*work in B*) = 3
utility(*work in C*) = 7

This results in the following preferences:

work in C > *work in A* > *work in B*

and consequently the following meaning:

meaning of workplace = C(Naomi) = (choices, preferences) = ({*A, B, C*}, {*C* > *B*, *C* > *A*, *A* > *B*})

Phil and Naomi notice that they share the preference *work in C* > *work in A* but Phil prefers B to C whereas Naomi prefers C to B. The meanings their workplace holds for them are partly shared and partly different which makes perfect sense as they experience it in partly similar and partly distinct ways. They conjecture that this is likely to be the case for all the employees: overlapping but not identical meanings. These assessments show that there could be room for some trade-offs and compromise across the firm, imperfect and somewhat arbitrary though they may be. Phil and Naomi realize that in this situation they must make a collective rather than an individual choice. Perhaps design C might be one shared optimal choice for everyone even if it is not Phil's top choice or that of others like him. They note the following tentative outcomes:

workplace → meaning for each employee → *work in A* → poorer effects on health and productivity
workplace → meaning for each employee → *work in C* → better effects on health and productivity

They could also engage an architect more formally to explore further options with more detailed specifications. So they create a proposal for the relevant committee based on a wider survey of all the employees' preferences, promising increased productivity and enhanced physical and mental well-being for everyone both individually and collectively. Phil's firm is now actively considering new designs.

Here we have used rational choice theory with its accompanying utility analyses as we did when Phil initially chose to walk to work in the previous chapter. We could as easily have used prospect theory instead with its relative gains and losses by measuring them from the existing reference point of working in A rather than using the absolute benefits and costs of rational decision-making. The results of the analysis would have been the same as before even though the numbers would have been slightly different. This is because of losses looming larger than corresponding gains or, in other words, because of loss aversion. More importantly, though, in this instance absolute magnitudes are more appropriate as the workplace staff are all consciously and explicitly trying to arrive at the optimal design and the biases that arise from reference points or the status quo are unlikely to intervene. In other words, in such deliberate choice situations, rationality is likely to prevail over irrationality because everyone involved engages in slow thinking rather than fast.

3.2 Anchoring

Consider the following two questions from Kahneman's *Thinking, Fast and Slow* that are put to Phil by his former roommate from college who is a psychologist.

(1) Was Gandhi more or less than 144 years old when he died?
(2) How old was Gandhi when he died?[1]

Even though the first question is a little absurd and Phil answers as we would expect, it unconsciously influences his answer—95 years—to the second question, making it significantly higher than he might have guessed otherwise. The correct answer is 78 years. Indeed, most experimental subjects give higher answers in this context than if they were asked the second question without such a context. This phenomenon is called *anchoring* and the first question serves as an anchor to the second. What happens is that the initial question primes us to expect a much older person via the associative machinery of the mind. We instinctively try to make the second answer coherent or compatible with the first question. Even though the first question mentioned a nonsensically high age we unconsciously bring our answer closer to it than we would have otherwise.[2]

In *Nudge*, Thaler and Sunstein observe that if a charity asks Phil or anyone else for amounts like $100, $250, $1000, $5000, and *other*, most people will likely give a much higher donation than if it asked for amounts like $50, $75, $100, $150. Typically, the more you ask for the more you get. The opening figure in many negotiations can influence the final result dramatically.[3]

What is common to these very different settings is that they involve our consideration in two stages. In such cases, the experience of the first stage invariably influences the outcome of the second stage even when the first stage is irrelevant to the second. If the first stage is chosen carefully, it can nudge people to desired actions in the second. As Thaler and Sunstein say, if a greater voter turnout is sought, the simplest way often is to ask the relevant community the day before the election if they intend to vote. This mere question can increase the participation by as much as 25%![4]

Phil's former roommate reveals to him that this kind of anchoring occurs in a wide variety of situations that intermix ideas and actions. In one experiment, college undergraduates were exposed to words indicative of old age such as *Florida, forgetful, bald, gray*, or *wrinkle*. They were then sent down the hall to do another experiment. Without revealing what the experimenters were doing, they measured the time it took the subjects to reach their destination. This was the purpose of the experiment. Their amazing finding was that after such an implicit exposure to ideas about the elderly (without any actual mention of the word "old"), the young undergraduates walked more slowly than their normal pace. None of them were aware that the words they had encountered had a common theme; they denied that their actions had been influenced by such an idea. As Kahneman points out, even reading this paragraph primes us to be momentarily slower in a subsequent action such as standing up to get a glass of water![5]

This influencing of actions by ideas has been acknowledged for a long time and is named the *ideomotor effect*. It also works in reverse wherein an action influences an idea. In a mirror image of the experiment above, young subjects were asked to walk at a much slower pace and it was then found that they responded more quickly to words like *forgetful, old*, and *lonely*. In other words, there is a reciprocity in the effects: if we are primed to think of the elderly, we act old, and acting old makes us more receptive to thoughts of old age.

None of these examples are directly about choices but they can be seen as such. For example, there are implicit choices involved in guessing Gandhi's age or making a donation or voting or walking fast or slow or responding more quickly to words suggesting age. The first stage in each situation anchors or nudges us toward a certain type of choice in the second. This kind of biasing violates invariance because the actions are generally different if the first stage is absent. This makes them irrational. In such situations, it is, as Kahneman says, our fast intuitive thinking that pushes us one way or another: no further theory like prospect theory is required to explain the action as it is more or less automatic.[6]

Can these insights be used by architects? We conjecture that they can—and in a variety of appropriately designed environments.

When Phil's office is being redesigned, he tells the architect about his newfound knowledge of anchoring.

After absorbing how it works, she creatively reasons through the following steps. First, suppose the layout of the various rooms serving different functions is organized in a manner that requires more walking to and fro and up and down—remember that Phil's company takes up two floors in the building. During the day the occupants will end up taking more steps and be pegged to a higher level of activity. This would constitute the first stage of the anchoring process. In the second stage, if this architectural analogy is to work, we should expect Phil and his colleagues to (at least unconsciously) entertain more *ideas* of continuing activity after they finish their work for the day. And these ideas would in some cases lead to actual physical activity such as going to the gym or playing tennis or squash.

The key underlying insight is the inverse of the ideomotor effect where we saw that walking very slowly primes people to respond more readily to ideas related to old age. In our architectural setting, the first stage would involve the office goers being subtly required to exert more as compared with the existing office plan where the design is optimized for the proximity of various related functions. The architect realizes this has to be done within reasonable limits (obviously) so that everyone's work can still be efficiently accomplished. Once Phil and his colleagues are set up to walk more, the principle of anchoring suggests that in the second stage they are likely to be receptive to ideas—and subsequent actions—of even more exercise. Thus, how the bathrooms, copying and other services, mailrooms, conference rooms, and even the individual offices are laid out can make a huge difference to not just the first-stage levels of activity but even to the second-stage consequences of this activity.

Indeed, it is a familiar experience for everyone that if we are relatively sedentary through the day, we are likely to want to persist in that inactive state, and if we are more active, we are likely to continue in that energetic mode. This is why Thaler and Sunstein say there is *no* neutral design.[7] Phil's existing workplace inhibits activity and the proposed workplace could stimulate it. Today many activity trackers that measure physical activity are available and the informal finding seems to be that within limits, the more we do the more we are likely to continue to do. In other words, there is a double effect: the occupants walk more indoors and later exert more elsewhere.

Not only this, there is also an unexpected bonus. If people are moving about outside their individual offices more, they are more likely to encounter their colleagues and this inevitably leads to a healthier social environment,

not to mention elevated moods and improved motivation. If the requirements of the previous section—such as natural light—are combined with
this new insight from anchoring, the overall design could make Phil's office
a very rewarding place to work.

Even when greater levels of activity are promoted within new and
enlightened office designs today, they seldom take into account a deeper
understanding of human behavior of the kind we are discussing. The general thinking is at best first-order whereas we are offering a second-order
intuition. This latter point may not have any particular effect on the actual
design but it does allow us to better evaluate the importance of promoting
such layouts worldwide because they have a second-order impact as well.

Part of such a new design's meaning is precisely a preference for something like going to the gym or playing tennis over simply heading home and
watching television, which is exactly the opposite with respect to the existing design. In section 3.1 we considered three alternative layouts: A, B, C.
There we found that C worked best for the whole office staff. If we therefore
ignore option B and simply contrast A (the existing design) with C, and
incorporate the lessons from the principle of anchoring into C, we find the
meaning of the workplace reinforced thus for the entire set of office workers:

$$\text{meaning of workplace} = C = (\text{choices, preferences}) = (\{A, C\}, \{C > A\})$$

While the meaning of the workplace is expressed as before in terms of a
choice of designs, we can also express the meaning of C itself as follows:

$$\text{meaning of } C = C = (\text{choices, preferences}) = (\{\textit{go home, play tennis}\},$$
$$\{\textit{play tennis} > \textit{go home}\})$$

That is, once C is implemented, it would hold this partial meaning for Phil
and his colleagues. The meaning is partial because there are other aspects
of meaning too: the additional benefits discussed in the previous section. As
we said earlier, the partial meaning of A is exactly the opposite:

$$\text{meaning of } A = C = (\text{choices, preferences}) = (\{\textit{go home, play tennis}\},$$
$$\{\textit{go home} > \textit{play tennis}\})$$

Going back to comparing alternative designs, we would once again have:

workplace $\rightarrow$ meaning for each employee $\rightarrow$ *work in A* $\rightarrow$ poorer health
and productivity
workplace $\rightarrow$ meaning for each employee $\rightarrow$ *work in C* $\rightarrow$ better health
and productivity

This time, the better effects on health and productivity would result from a combination of rational effects and irrational effects, from the benefits of natural light and related things and from the benefits of anchoring used to the staff's positive advantage. Once again, it is important to point out that the analysis above is *theoretical*. Whether anchoring works in this way in this particular architectural setting remains to be empirically tested.

We now turn to a very different kind of application of anchoring to show how versatile it can be. This is the design of residential neighborhoods.

If there are multi-family buildings with a mix of land uses within a small enough radius to constitute a neighborhood—the mix involving all kinds of services like grocery stores, cafés, retail outlets, bank branches, gyms, pharmacies and dry cleaners and locksmiths and sundry other conveniences—this kind of setting can once again subtly get people to engage in many small errands on a more or less daily basis. The alternative configuration would be to require getting into a car to obtain a small necessity like a carton of milk.

The first kind of mixed-use neighborhood would also provide an active scene on the streets with people milling about, stopping to make small talk with neighbors, and generally spending more time outdoors. This sort of environment lifts spirits as much as it sparks movement. And then, via the principle of anchoring, this first-stage increased activity can potentially

Figure 3.4 A mixed-use neighborhood

galvanize people into going for more walks. Walking provides not just physical exercise but it connects Phil to the city in many unexpected ways: with people, with the landmarks of the city, with a whole sense of being part of something larger than himself, which, as is well known, is one of the keys to happiness. This enables us to write:

> meaning of mixed-use neighborhood = ({*stay home, go for walks*}, {*go for walks* > *stay home*})
> mixed-use neighborhood → meaning → *walk* → better health

Naturally, there are tradeoffs involved at every step but that is what going from theory to practice inevitably means. That is why, when an architect compares alternative designs for a neighborhood, she cannot blithely write:

> meaning of neighborhood = C = ({*mixed use, single use*}, {*mixed use* > *single use*})

Mixed-use neighborhoods are not *always* preferred to single-use neighborhoods because there are always other factors that also matter. It is rare in architecture to be able to establish such *universal* "theorems" and so one should not expect to. As we said earlier, theorists always need to go back and forth between abstractions and the total concrete situation which is always very complex.

In any case, one can see that many if not all of these choice-theoretic insights can inform design at various scales, from interiors to exteriors, and they can all work in concert, creating places that nourish life in multiple ways. In both Phil's workplace and his neighborhood, we can also always add art and sculpture that invite reflection by momentarily getting passersby to bracket the everyday world in order to contemplate alternative possibilities for life itself. That is, art will not only inspire aesthetic responses but can also lead us to see the world afresh. When we do this habitually as an integral part of our day, anchoring can reinforce it by priming us to reorient our lives in more fulfilling ways. Our health consists not only of physical activity and moods but equally of perceptions and thoughts.

3.3 Availability

In some ways *availability* is the most obvious and ubiquitous bias people show even though, as Kahneman points out, its details can be quite subtle to analyze.[8] If someone has just read about a plane crash in a newspaper, they are likely to estimate a higher probability for the risks involved in flying. Because people hear so much about corruption among politicians, they are likely to think politicians are inherently more prone to such behavior. And so on. Essentially, we tend to judge the frequency of events and the size of categories based on how easily their instances come to mind—how *available* they are.

This availability heuristic can be re-expressed in terms of choice problems by noting that people are, for example, more likely to buy earthquake insurance after learning about an earthquake in their area. This kind of action is irrational as a result of the choice behavior changing based on the relative availability of an instance even though the choice situation is the same. When people choose between, say, buying earthquake insurance or not, the earlier decision may have been to opt out, but when an earthquake occurs nearby, one is likely to say yes even though the actual risk or probability of earthquakes has not changed. In other words, the principle of invariance is breached.

Thaler and Sunstein give an example of this in situations where no uncertainty is present unlike the examples above. Consider two ways of arranging the food in a self-serve restaurant. One is to place carrots at eye level—where they are more "available"—and desserts at a lower level. The other way is exactly the opposite with desserts at eye level and carrots at the lower level. In the first situation, the customers are likely to unconsciously opt for carrots many more times than they would have otherwise. In the second situation, the desserts will be selected more often. That is, the choices made are different even though the choice sets are the same. Indeed, in an actual experiment students in a high school cafeteria chose healthier food by as much as 25% when it was made visually more accessible. These are occasions where the tendency to irrational behavior has been used for students' benefit: they have been nudged into making a healthier choice.[9]

Any such placement of food which makes one item more available than another will have some consequence for health—for better or for worse. And this is true of a large variety of choices we all face on a daily basis, not just of food. In grocery stores and other similar venues, marketers have known for a long time that they can sway people into impulsively buying gossip magazines and trinkets by simply placing them prominently at the checkout counter where they can be seen while waiting in line. These are items customers may never buy otherwise but they succumb when they are made available. The lesson to be learned is that we have an easy opportunity to influence people to make choices that enhance their lives rather than diminish them.

Theoretically speaking, it may be possible to analyze availability in terms of the gains and losses of prospect theory but it may be overkill and may not capture accurately what is going on when someone yields to such a bias. So we will just accept this empirical insight at face value and see how it may be extended to our architectural setting.

As we have seen from our foregoing consideration of Phil's two-level workplace inside a high-rise, the architect was hired to provide better access to natural light as well as to make use of anchoring to stimulate greater activity. In this very different setting, there is an opportunity to get people to climb up stairs rather than take the elevator more often than not. The stairs are like the carrots because they boost our health and the elevator is like the dessert because it does not improve our health and may in fact worsen it. All the architect needs to do is make the stairs more available.

In the current layout of Phil's office, the existing stairwell of the high-rise is unattractive and relatively hidden and meant mainly as a fire escape. Leaving things as they are would result in most of the staff taking the elevators. The architect's other alternative is to design an attractive internal staircase that is prominently placed in the center of the floor. Because of its greater availability—made so not only by its location but also by its striking visual and tactile appearance—Phil and his colleagues are more likely in this scenario to go up and down these internal stairs in an easy burst of physical activity, perhaps even stopping to exchange small talk with other workers from time to time, an added benefit. With this latter offering, not only does the physical layout become more compelling architecturally, binding the two levels as it does, the whole office generates a certain social

Figure 3.5 Office environment with internal staircase

cohesion and activates more endorphins among the staff. Regular behavior of this kind is known to dramatically reduce the risk of stroke and provide many other related benefits as well.

We can once again encode the meanings evoked in the following way:

meaning of internal staircase = ({*climb up, take elevator*}, {*climb up* > *take elevator*})
internal staircase → meaning → *climb up* → better health

These meanings and ensuing actions would generally be true of everyone in Phil's workplace and so such a plan could easily be contemplated. However, as there are monetary costs involved in creating a duplex in addition to other considerations, the architect would need to consult Phil's office before assuming that internal stairs are preferable to the existing arrangement, that is, before taking it for granted that:

meaning of staircase = *C* = ({*internal, external*}, {*internal* > *external*})

This element of a stairway deserves a renewed focus far beyond Phil's office. Earlier buildings were low-rise and there were no elevators so stairs were often a prominent aspect of a building's entrance and lobby. They did not only fulfill functions but created an independent source of visual and multi-sensory interest. The rise of multistory buildings together with the introduction of elevators and escalators has unfortunately led to staircases being relegated to the rear of a lobby and to making them completely unattractive so that even the most motivated person would rarely choose to climb upstairs. This has in turn exacerbated the deleterious effects of sedentary lifestyles. Newer buildings, especially public ones, are beginning to take this unintended and negative health effect into account but there is clearly a long way to go. If such situations are better understood in light of the choice-theoretic principle of availability, it may in fact induce architects and others to incorporate this insight into the role of stairways into all their designs so that it becomes a commonplace feature of buildings. It is in fact an opportunity to create more aesthetic interest in lobbies and a multitude of other places.

There are many building types that naturally lend themselves to this kind of "innovation": museums and other cultural establishments, many university and school buildings, the interiors of some offices, houses in suburbs and contiguous areas, airports, train stations, and, in fact, practically any building that qualifies as a low-rise. Even for high-rises, making staircases more conspicuous and attractive may not be a waste because at least people who have to access the lower floors could benefit.

Figure 3.6 A prominently placed staircase

The placement and relative appeal of staircases, that is, their availability vis-à-vis elevators or escalators is likely to be an easy architectural intervention in many settings. Practically everyone is faced with such choices in public and private buildings. While it is impractical to try to nudge people to climb stairs in even a moderately tall building, there are still many opportunities to encourage them to climb a couple of flights instead of taking an elevator. The meanings generated in all such instances involve a choice between taking the stairs or the elevator or escalator and the different semi-conscious preferences induced depending on how the architect presents the options in terms of their relative accessibility.

We can write a slightly modified pair of equations for such situations as follows:

meaning of prominent staircase = ({*climb up, take elevator*}, {*climb up > take elevator*})

prominent staircase → meaning → *climb up* → better health

The second set of availability examples has more to do with planning and zoning than with architecture per se but they show how thoughtfully locating certain sorts of elements in certain types of places can make them more or less available and thereby induce healthful behavior. For example, if fast food restaurants are restricted to stay away from schools by at least half a mile if not a mile and if restaurants offering more nutritious fare are encouraged to situate themselves closer to schools, this would inevitably lead to students eating better simply owing to the greater proximity of healthier food. Again, this is no different from placing carrots at eye level but it involves the location of physical establishments, not food itself. This sort of regulatory insight applies not just to restaurants but also public libraries, various related educational institutions and centers, and even movie houses showing a wider range of cinema so that the curiosity of students is not only triggered but also quenched. Similar to this kind of strategy is the placement of water fountains close to playgrounds so that children opt to drink water rather than soda from a vending machine. It should be straightforward to see how our notion of meaning and interpretation extends to all these cases.

A slightly different and therefore third set of examples involves the placement of public art, something we mentioned in the previous section although it really belongs to this category of availability because it is the easy sighting of the art that matters. Likewise art can also be made available in the interiors of offices and in the lobbies of buildings. In addition to the benefits identified earlier, art invites reflection and stimulates us to think

Figure 3.7 A water fountain close to a playground

Figure 3.8 Public art

out of the box. Large public artworks can even forge community involvement in neighborhoods as has happened with certain well-known instances in many cities. Apart from such direct effects, art can transform an interior or exterior space in unexpected ways and this larger embedding space then acquires a power to affect us even more. From the point of view of choice, Phil or others can either notice or ignore a sculpture when walking by and the corresponding choice problem becomes the meaning of the artwork and its surrounding space.

The key thing to bear in mind when thinking about how to use availability is that as we said earlier there are no neutral designs. Every arrangement has some consequence for health, whether positive or negative, and whether it has been consciously thought through or not. So it behooves architects and public officials to mindfully organize layouts and plans in ways that promote health rather than destroy it. Just as it has become second nature for architects to make doorways wide enough for passage and windows large enough for light and air, so this kind of orientation to health must become second nature in ways that don't make it an afterthought but an integral part of design thinking.

3.4 The Cost of Zero Cost

Just as with availability, we are all familiar with the zero cost principle. All it says is that we are all irrationally susceptible to things that are free or have *zero cost*. Everyone has been to conferences and brought back pens and notepads simply because they were free. Many of us may have no real use for these items but even the more restrained among us succumb. As some of us subsequently realize, these free items carry a small *hidden* cost that is definitely *not* zero: they create unwanted clutter in our homes and offices. In other words, these items that have a zero monetary cost sometimes have a non-monetary cost that could be small or large.

Ariely and others have pointed out that when we have a choice of buying a product from a range of alternatives, the rational thing to do is to choose the item with the highest net benefit.[10] That is, for each item we evaluate its utility = benefit − cost and choose the one with the highest utility. But many experiments and observations show that we do not simply subtract monetary costs from benefits when the prices are zero. It appears that we also tend to *irrationally* inflate the benefits of free products. That is, if the same item has a benefit of x when it costs one cent, its benefit would appear much greater than x when it is offered at no cost. So in the first situation we may not buy the item but in the second we would likely choose it even though the choices are effectively the same. Once again, invariance is flouted.

An explanation of this attitude to free things is that we seem to derive some special momentary pleasure from their being free. As a result, we magnify their perceived benefit and react *disproportionately* to such offers—even if there are other non-monetary costs involved. These other costs are either not perceived clearly or appear less onerous than the corresponding exaggerated benefits.

Here is a true story from Ariely's book cited earlier. The world's largest bookseller—Amazon—offers free shipping if you buy books worth more than a certain amount. The first thing many readers may be dimly aware of is the number of times they themselves bought an additional at best half-desired book just to qualify for free shipping. But there is more. Amazon in France initially did not offer fully free shipping but instead charged a single franc for a high enough purchase order. They found that most customers did not increase their buying just to avail of the negligible but nonzero shipping fee. Later the French branch dropped the shipping cost to zero and, *voilà*, there was a dramatic increase in revenues. Even a tiny change from one franc to zero francs made a huge difference in the behavior of customers. To repeat, it appears that people derive some special pleasure from getting something for free and this increases its value to such an extent that they may end up incurring costs they regret later.[11]

It is not true, however, that all free items have partially undesirable con-sequences. Sometimes we do genuinely need that pen or notepad or even that book, and then our actions are smart rather than foolish. Like the other principles we have looked at so far, the zero cost principle is double-edged and can be used not only for private gain at the expense of others but also for the public good.

Interestingly, such Janus-faced instantiations occur frequently in archi-tectural settings as well. Phil is fortunate to have two free plazas not far from his workplace to choose from during his lunch hour. He likes to bring his lunch to one of these—call it A—rather than the other—call it B—and watch the world go by as he eats. Now that he has gotten involved in the design of his office interior, he has begun to take a keener interest in his sur-roundings and to reflect on why certain places work better than others and in what particular ways.

He observes that A is almost at street level—he only has to climb up a couple of steps—and that he can see the street and its goings-on from inside the plaza and vice versa. That is, passersby glance inward at the plaza and take in the scene of people sitting alone or in clusters, nibbling, and talking. The other plaza, B, has a nice green hedge along its perimeter but it blocks this two-way view and makes the space a quieter, more private enclave. One

Figure 3.9 Plaza A

Figure 3.10 Plaza B

also has to go up several steps to get to its more elevated level. He surmises that most people prefer to be with others and occasionally even strike up conversations with strangers and generally partake of the city's bustle in a comfortable, even idle way. Not only does this create a kind of downtime but it also connects them to a wider world.

The second thing Phil notices is that plaza A is smaller than plaza B with denser clusters of movable chairs and tables and benches in the midst of greenery. B has ample shrubbery but it is a larger space with spread-out sitting places that are part of the immovable stone of the plaza itself. Its scale is less human and so it intangibly seems a little cold and formal and even forbidding despite the fact that it has been artfully designed. A seems more like a concrete *place* and B seems more like a somewhat abstract *space*.

As a result, A occasions greater human contact and social interaction even when no words are exchanged—the chatter of people is easily heard in the air. The movability of the chairs and other furniture gives A a more casual feel, even allowing people to shift positions more readily as they sit alone or with friends.

As the urbanist William Whyte pointed out not so long ago, places like A that are free are usually more successful in attracting people.[12] They generate a subtler kind of healthful enjoyment, a plenitude of being, and sometimes even create a sense of belonging and community. On the other hand, all too often, when there are overly large open plazas like B, visually separated from the activity of the street with few comfortable places to sit and move, the result can be indifference, anomie, and alienation. Although Phil does at times eat at nearby restaurants and cafés to vary his experiences and his food, the zero cost of both the plazas is an initially inviting alternative. Indeed, as we have demonstrated, it is disproportionately so, attracting users more than even very low-cost fast food eateries in the same way that the French customers of Amazon were enticed by its sudden switch to free shipping. These users inflate the plazas' perceived benefit. Unfortunately, like Amazon's free shipping, plaza B comes with a hidden cost: Phil feels less revitalized for the day. So it is A he frequents, as do many others who work in the same neighborhood, some of whom he even recognizes on occasion.

To review, Phil has three choices: a nonzero-cost café and two zero-cost plazas. By the principle of zero cost, he is likely to initially prefer the free plazas A and B more often than not. Through repeated experience, he has realized that A refreshes him more than B and so he chooses A over B. In economic language, although B is free it comes with a hidden cost whereas A is free and offers additional benefits rather than hidden costs. We have deliberately introduced two free items in this example to contrast situations having wholly positive effects with those where hidden costs diminish the returns to the user. Indeed, Phil may find B so depleting that he might even prefer the café to B. This is because his choices are made many times over an extended period. We can describe this situation succinctly as follows:

meaning of office neighborhood = ({*plaza A, plaza B, café*}, {*plaza A >
    café > plaza B*})
office neighborhood → meaning → *plaza A* → better health

Few office neighborhoods are like Phil's with a choice of two free plazas and this allows him to opt for the healthier one. Many people have access only to one suboptimal plaza like B which they are inveigled into using temporarily and then they have to suffer the hidden costs of its zero cost. They are likely to realize through multiple experiences that they would be better off eating in a restaurant. In such situations, there are one of two possible outcomes. Either the uninspiring but free plaza will be relatively deserted like plaza B or those who cannot afford to eat daily at a nearby café will be forced to suffer its unhealthy impact.

Architects along with developers and city officials need to be aware that the free spaces they create possess disproportionate power over even inexpensive delis and could encumber their users with repeated unhealthful experiences. With the right knowledge, the very irrationality of users could be turned to their advantage by designing positive experiences instead of negative ones, that is, instead of ones that are encumbered with hidden costs.

3.5 Nonlinearity

Despite its somewhat technical name, nonlinearity is a straightforward concept.[13]

Consider a somewhat fortunate occurrence for Phil. He receives $50 from an unexpected source. This results in some satisfaction. Then he is given a second amount of $50 by the same source. Will he experience the same degree of satisfaction the second time? If the answer is yes, it means the values he derives from such successive gifts are *linear*. However, numerous experiments with real money show that these values are in fact *nonlinear* and tend to taper off with each subsequent gift.[14] A third such amount would mean relatively less than the second just as the second means less than the first. Tversky and Kahneman's prospect theory explains these diminishing returns in a very natural way.[15]

Recall from the last chapter how we considered Tom's job offers and his preference for the status quo and that prospect theory does not evaluate the absolute options an agent faces but measures them as deviations from a neutral reference point. These deviations can be positive or negative and are called gains and losses. The theory translates the gains and losses into values. The relationship between values on the one hand and gains or losses on the other is given by an *S* curve shown in Figure 3.11. Gains and losses are plotted on the *X*-axis and values on the *Y*-axis and the origin (0, 0) is the reference point.

To understand Phil's reaction to the gifts, look at the shape of the curve. It is concave on its positive side and convex on its negative side, which means that it flattens out as it moves away from the origin. This implies, for example, that the difference in value between gains of $0 and $50 is greater than the difference between gains of $50 and $100.[16] This flattening out on both sides is what makes it nonlinear.

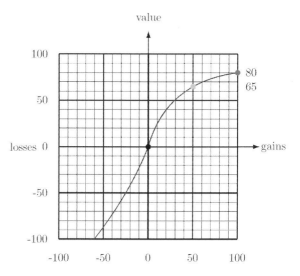

Figure 3.11 How nonlinearity works

Phil's reference point (0, 0) is shown by a dot at the origin of the graph. The first $50 he gets would be represented as a gain of 50 on the X-axis. As can be seen, the value he derives from it is 65 units as shown by the dot at (50, 65). His net value is 65 − 0 = 65 or, spelled out a little more formally:

value(reference point)   = 0
value(after receiving $50)   = 65
added value(after receiving $50) = 65 − 0 = 65

The second amount of $50 would be represented by a total gain of $100 on the X-axis. If his experience was linear, it would imply that his value doubles from 65 to 130 and the added value would be 130 − 65 = 65 as before. This is not so. As we have just seen, his gains flatten out and the second $50 only gives him a total value of 80 units as shown by the dot at (100, 80) in the same figure. This in turn implies:

value(after receiving the first $50)   = 65
value(after receiving the second $50)   = 80
added value(after receiving the second $50) = 80 − 65 = 15

The second gain of $50 yields a smaller added value than the first. This is the phenomenon of nonlinearity. These diminishing returns are common sense and do not apply only to monetary gains. A scoop of ice cream means more to Phil before he has eaten any scoops than after he has already had one. That is, the difference in value between one scoop and none is greater than the difference in value between two scoops and one or, alternatively, the first scoop is more satisfying than the second. Exactly the same analysis as before applies with a scoop of ice cream taken as a gain of 50 units.

Now we can look at architectural analogues of this behavioral pattern. Recall that Phil's office neighborhood has two free plazas. They can be viewed as similar to the two scoops of ice cream or the two gifts of $50. When the neighborhood got its first plaza, everyone around Phil gravitated to it. Its value was high. It is like the first gift of $50. But when the second plaza is added, it does not mean as much. This is because the *S* curve flattens out and the new gain has a lower added value and is like Phil's receiving the second free gift of $50. The impact on the health and emotions of Phil's office community is not twice as great with two plazas because the value relationship is concave rather than linear. See Figure 3.12 where each of the two plazas is shown as providing successive gains of 50 units, the first yielding an added value of $65 - 0 = 65$ as before and the second yielding an added value of only $80 - 65 = 15$.

Consider a slightly more complex scenario with two residential buildings, one in Phil's mixed-use neighborhood and the other in a residential neighborhood. In the first case, suppose Phil has access to a neighborhood

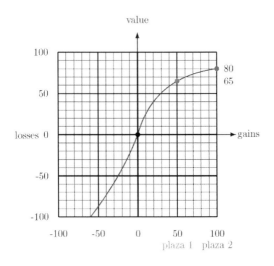

Figure 3.12 How nonlinearity works with the two plazas

Figure 3.13 A second plaza like plaza A remains relatively unused

gym he can easily walk to. Should his building provide an in-house gym? It could but its full value will not be realized as Phil and his fellow residents already have an easily accessible gym. This is like the situation above with the two plazas replaced by the two gyms as shown in Figure 3.14. While the first neighborhood gym added a value of 65, the second building gym would add a value of only 15.

The corresponding calculations are as before but we show them again to ease the contrast between the two cases. For the first neighborhood gym:

value(reference point) = 0
value(first gym)   = 65
added value(first gym) = 65 – 0 = 65

And for the second building gym:

value(first gym)   = 65
value(second gym)   = 80
added value(second gym) = 80 – 65 = 15

In the second instance of the residential neighborhood, the external gym is quite a distance away and residents have to drive to it. This makes access

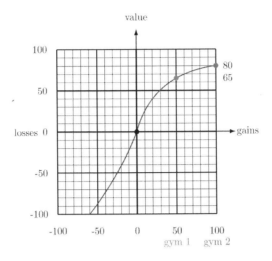

Figure 3.14 How nonlinearity works in a mixed-use neighborhood

Figure 3.15 An in-house gym

cumbersome and the gain derived from it is much smaller, say 10 units, and so its value is also much smaller at about 24 as shown by the dot at (10, 24) in Figure 3.16.

In this situation, should an in-house gym be contemplated? The *S* curve suggests that its value would be considerably higher because the gain from

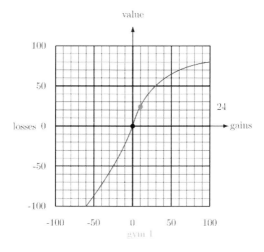

Figure 3.16 How nonlinearity works in a residential neighborhood

this second in-house gym could be taken as 50 units as before and it would take the total gain to $10 + 50 = 60$. This yields a value of 70 as shown by the dot at (60, 70) in Figure 3.17.

It is interesting to see the different calculations in this second case. For the first external gym that residents have to drive to:

value(reference point) = 0
value(first gym)   = 24
added value(first gym) = 24 – 0 = 24

And for the second in-house gym that might be considered:

value(first gym)   = 24
value(second gym)   = 70
added value(second gym) = 70 – 24 = 46

So the added value with the first external gym was just 24 but the added value with the second in-house gym is much higher at 46. So in this residential neighborhood context it makes sense to seriously consider an in-house gym as against the mixed-use neighborhood where it seems unnecessary.

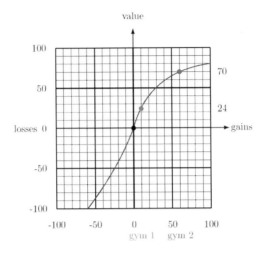

Figure 3.17 How nonlinearity works in a residential neighborhood

Incidentally, these considerations also show the flexibility of the apparatus we are using. While successive gains of equal magnitudes (e.g. 50 units)
show diminishing returns, successive gains of unequal magnitudes (e.g. 10
and 50 units) could, in the right circumstances, show increasing returns.
It all depends on the particular cases being examined; prospect theory's *S*
curve can handle most of them.

The principle of nonlinearity provides guidance for city planners and
developers to distribute various facilities among more neighborhoods to
maximize the benefits of their investments. This simple insight into how
value is perceived nonlinearly can be applied at all the levels of the built
environment from single rooms through apartments and offices all the way
to cities and even entire regions. It is an added tool for architects to have as
part of their design strategy when they plan not only plazas, buildings, and
neighborhoods but also other features across built spaces.

3.6 Representativeness

We often make snap judgments about people, things, and events being
of a certain type based on a few *representative* cues. These cues offer at
best partial evidence but they make us jump to rationally unwarranted
conclusions.

The following is an adaptation of a famous example presented by Kahneman and Tversky.[17] Imagine Phil is part of an experiment and is told

Linda is a thirty-one-year-old very bright single woman who majored in philosophy and was concerned about social justice in her student days. The participants are then asked to decide whether it is more likely Linda is a bank teller or a feminist bank teller. Phil immediately classifies her as a feminist bank teller. Even groups trained in probabilistic thinking make this choice.

Upon reflection it is clear that her being a bank teller is more likely than her being a feminist bank teller because there are many more bank tellers than feminist bank tellers (just as there are many more Americans than Indian Americans in the world). Phil knows that this makes being just a bank teller more probable than being a feminist bank teller (just as it would make being an American more probable than being an Indian American from the pool of all the people in the world), but the *stereotypical* description of Linda traps him into thinking otherwise.

As should be evident, this kind of stereotype-based thinking is common. It involves categorizing things one way or another based on misleading cues. Consider a slightly different scenario. If we do not mention Linda's being single and being concerned about social justice to Phil, he is less likely to be mistaken and more likely to think correctly about the classification. In other words, in both cases, the choices are the same, but because different attributes are highlighted in each case, Phil judges differently. With this bias too, therefore, just as with anchoring and availability, it is the principle of invariance that is infringed, making his action irrational.

How could we adapt this to our architectural setting?

Suppose it's a summer morning and Phil has some official work to do. He has to go to a public building for it. As he approaches the building, attuned to his architectural surroundings as he has increasingly become, he immediately notices an architrave and pediment on the façade in an otherwise modern design. He is struck by the aura of solemnity and grandeur it conveys and for him it also reflects the governmental activity inside.

How exactly does the connection between the classical elements and their meanings inform Phil of the building's historical mission? As we said, most of its attributes are modern. This allows the architrave and pediment to stand out because they are different. They function as a stereotype for Phil and for most visitors, often unconsciously evoking a vaguely distinguished past. That is, they are representative of classical times. Even though the majority of attributes point to a more prosaic context, the historical cues convince us of an association with stateliness and splendor. All it takes to accomplish this is a few significant and *representative* elements.

Such devices can be used whether or not the corresponding meanings are warranted, that is, they can be used honestly or dishonestly. For example,

Figure 3.18 A public building with classical elements

white walls with modern art and furniture in a corporate setting may convey efficiency even if the business housed in it is managed poorly. Fortunately for Phil, his own office's design cues genuinely match the quality of the work the company does. Nevertheless, this possibility of misleading users through the judicious use of a few elements is a significant architectural fact.

Usually, the connection between built forms and their meanings is asserted as if it is automatic. Our analysis digs deeper and explains how some meanings might emerge via the heuristic of representativeness.

So far we have looked at the application of this idea to architectural meaning generally. What about its relevance for Phil's health? Before he moved to his current mixed-use residential neighborhood, he lived in a less central one that lacked the resources of the present location. As he reflects back on it one Sunday afternoon, he realizes that despite this dearth he never felt deprived or dispirited. Why is that? It comes to him in a flash: it is because the municipality always provided all the simple things like proper street lighting and clean pavements. These features worked in a double way. First, they ensured that certain basic functions were served. In addition, they signaled a feeling of normalcy. This happened despite there being no public art or sculpture, no restful rows of trees, no vibrant *life* around and about. This low cost strategy worked because a few stereotypes such as adequate

Figure 3.19 A corporate setting conveying efficiency

Figure 3.20 A residential neighborhood signaling relative healthfulness

Figure 3.21 A cheerful doctor's clinic

lighting and cleanliness overrode and prevailed over the environment's drabness to some degree and managed to sustain the mood of its residents.

In such situations, representativeness satisfies by creating an *illusion* of healthfulness. A doctor's clinic may not be the most cheerful place but appropriate colors and furniture can reduce the stress of waiting. And, as we have seen, cities often have scarce resources to simultaneously upgrade all neighborhoods.

The key to understanding representativeness in such instances is the communicating of things as better than they may actually be and keeping our spirits up in hard times.

3.7 Framing

In recent decades the idea of framing has become widely known in several fields as well as in popular discourse.

Suppose Phil is considering an optional surgical procedure and asks his doctor for some more information about it. His doctor may say either of the following:

(1) 90% of the patients survive the procedure.
(2) 10% of the patients do not survive the procedure.

With (1) Phil is likely to want to go ahead with the surgery as it seems reasonably safe. With (2) he might hesitate or opt out altogether. This is despite the fact that the information conveyed by both statements is exactly the same. What Phil immediately considers with the first one is his chances of survival and better health afterwards—a gain. With the second one, he immediately considers his chances of death—a loss. As we know from prospect theory, losses loom larger than equivalent gains and so Phil exaggerates the risk of death. This is loss aversion, and when the risk is communicated to him, it makes him reject the surgery. If he were to stop and think, he would realize that a 90% chance of success and a 10% chance of failure imply the same risk. They represent the same uncertain situation. The difference lies just in what is explicit and what is implicit in the two ways of communicating it.

When Phil chooses in these contrary ways, it is the principle of invariance that is transgressed: his choices are the same in both situations and so are the risks, but in one he says yes and in the other he says no because of the different ways in which the information is *framed*. This makes Phil's behavior irrational.

Framing is about the manner of presentation of a choice to an agent. All human communication involves some *way* of presenting what we wish to convey and this is the heart of the idea. Different formulations of the same facts can lead to different actions because the person is guided by the description rather than the real option. He does not pause and work things out because slow, deliberate thinking is hard. A doctor could present the same statistics to Phil in two different ways and influence his choice for or against the procedure. Now it should be possible to understand why framing is so widely known. Though it is subtle, its impact is everywhere around us, in large matters and small.

Interestingly, Phil's example above is adapted from an actual experiment the economist Arrow[18] discusses based on work by Tversky and Kahneman. In this case, it wasn't a patient like Phil who faced the choice but experienced surgeons. The amazing finding was that even doctors succumbed to different ways of framing medical choices. When told the chance of survival was 90%, some 80% of surgeons recommended surgery. However, when told the chance of death was 10%, only 50% recommended surgery. In other words, even surgeons reacted differently to different but equivalent descriptions. They, too, violated the principle of invariance and behaved irrationally.

Another way framing can work is by changing the reference point from which gains and losses are measured. An optimist sees the glass as half full because his reference point is an empty glass whereas a pessimist sees the same glass as half empty because his reference point is a full glass. Presenting the same state of the world in equivalent but different ways by making different aspects explicit, a framed situation can nudge people toward one kind of decision over another.

A perfectly rational agent simply sees the glass neutrally without any reference point influencing him because for him it is the actual situation that matters. When Shakespeare's Juliet says that a rose by any other name would smell as sweet, she is clear-eyed and does not confuse Romeo's family name with who he is as a human being, but most of us filter reality through how it is described in words. We tend to confuse language and reality, words and things.

Can this ubiquitous power of framing be turned to our advantage? In the present context of design inducing healthy actions, there are many instances where architecture is accompanied by some signage. There is then a framing of some element of the built environment that can tilt the agent toward one kind of behavior rather than another. Figure 3.22 shows an example designed by the New York City Department of Health and Mental Hygiene that prompts people to take the stairs. We analyze how this sign might work below.

One day Phil arrives by subway at Grand Central Station in New York. Usually, he steps onto the escalator for an easy ride. But today the sign in Figure 3.22 catches his eye. The attractive design strategically mounted on a wall at eye level prompts him to consider not only how he would gain in health but also how he could play his part in saving energy and preserving the environment. All these positive features become explicit in his mind in a matter of seconds and, impulsively, he chooses the stairs. In this way, the

Figure 3.22 An example of framing in architecture

Figure 3.23 Stair prompts

principle of framing suggests that he—and countless others—would take the stairs more often, assuming other things are equal.

As with the surgical procedure example, Phil's choices before the sign was put up and after are the same: the stairs or the escalator. His personal gain and the environmental gain are also the same in both situations. But without the signage, his gain remains implicit and so he climbs up less often on average. Again, Phil's behavior is different in otherwise identical choice situations and so, as before, the principle of invariance is defied and his action is irrational.

In terms of architectural interpretation, we can say that the two meanings are different:

> meaning of stairway without sign = ({*climb up, take escalator*}, {*take escalator* > *climb up*})
> meaning of stairway with sign = ({*climb up, take escalator*}, {*climb up* > *take escalator*})

and therefore:

> stairway without sign → meaning → *take escalator* → poorer health and environment
> stairway with sign → meaning → *climb up* → better health and environment

Such meanings and ensuing actions would generally be true of everyone at the subway station and so such an inducement could easily be contemplated by the city. We might even make a more general statement from an architectural viewpoint:

> meaning of stairway = C = ({*with sign, without sign*}, {*with sign* > *without sign*})

When such effects are extended to other suitable places where stairways occur, taking care not to make such exhortations too intrusive, they are likely to have a significant impact not only on the health of the city's inhabitants and medical costs but even on energy consumption and the environment.

It may seem that we have merely used an existing intervention already conceived by New York City. What have we added to it? Most likely the designers of the signage adopted a commonsensical orientation to persuading people to use the stairs more often. They probably did not think of it in terms of a choice problem that users face daily and probably did not make the alternatives and preferences too explicit. Our analysis allows us to explain why the strategy works. At some level, such prompts appear straightforward but it is only when one understands the underlying dynamics of choice that such initiatives can be confidently applied in many settings.

Informational and motivational messages can be culturally fine-tuned to a building's likely users. For example, in some places there could be multilingual messages or signs that point out health benefits such as calorie expenditures, weight control, or even just convenience. Larger fonts could ease things for the elderly, and so on. There could even be piped music along a stairway as this makes the upward journey pleasanter.

So far the insight we have offered into the phenomenon of framing is relatively mundane. Some may even find its adaptation to architecture a bit literal and unexciting. We now deepen and expand its scope to show its full power.

Look at Figure 3.23 more closely. Part of its appeal is linguistic and direct. But another part of its appeal is visual and indirect. First, the sign is a fresh green, the color of healthfulness whether it is in the context of the human body or the environment. Second, the white font and image stands out in a sharp and distinctive contrast against the green background. Third, the stairs and ascending figure are depicted in a stylized way that can refer to any person and the relevant climbing action is captured visually as well. Lastly, there is a pleasing aesthetic of simplicity that allows communication with just a glance even if Phil does not stop to read the entire text.

This sketch of how all aspects of the sign work together to spur healthy action should immediately suggest many architectural possibilities. After all, *utterances* are not just verbal, they can be visual and tactile as well. Architecture's many styles and forms and elements are all opportunities for framing responses by users. Indeed, whether it has been named as such or not, framing has been an essential part of architecture from the very beginning because every design evokes choice problems with some bias toward one action or another. Again, there is no neutral architecture.

For example, when there are large buildings the architect has to decide whether to create proportional spaces and façades that provide a human scale through appropriate ornamentation, materials, and related design elements. Many modern skyscrapers lack this and can be alienating as is well known. On the other hand, many traditional buildings feel warm and comfortable if not welcoming despite their monumental size. These different effects are the result of nothing but different types of framing. The particular choices may be understated ones such as wondering whether to linger in the relevant space or not. The range of impact that the environments we inhabit has on us cannot be overestimated. It is staggeringly huge. Every built form affects our well-being and health in subtly emotional and often ineffable ways.

A simpler example relates to how appropriate landscaping can more directly connect us to nature. We have already discussed how free plazas work. Playgrounds can encourage children's interest in and contact with nature by the use of appropriate colors and forms, associating them with their ecosystem and fostering a sense of stewardship toward it. Proximity to nature has also been known to improve the calm and balance of adults.

We have also considered other environments such as streets and offices and neighborhoods. Each of these points to occasions where framing can operate through the relevant architectural elements themselves, not just through signage. Once one begins to see such framing everywhere, it becomes clear that framing is not just an ordinary principle of behavioral economics, it is a kind of *meta* principle that subsumes many of the other principles we have looked at such as anchoring, availability, zero cost, nonlinearity, representativeness, relativity, status quo bias, and more. All of the latter are *particular* modes of framing—via a two-stage process, making something prominent or free, exploiting the concavity and convexity of our satisfactions, using stereotypical elements, introducing new options, exploiting reference points and loss aversion, and so on. Framing includes all of these and more.

Not all applications of framing have to do with health. It is a means to spark one kind of response over another, whether that response has to do with concrete personal meanings via choice problems or abstract impersonal ones via other means. There is, in a sense, a whole new way to see material and ornament and style through the lens of framing. What the idea clarifies is one *mechanism* through which architectural languages work. Writers on architecture have often tried to identify the kinds of meanings and effects different buildings and other forms evoke, but they are seldom able to pin down *how* such evocation occurs except to claim that this configuration of elements has that effect. This leaves a fundamental aspect of architecture unexplained to the present day.

Although there is a great deal more to architectural communication than framing, it is certainly one of the important ways through which meanings are created and transmitted to users. The idea allows us to develop a partial theory of architecture and its components such as materials and ornamentation and style that transcends our current goal of addressing health. This broader possibility shows that health is in fact an integral part of architecture contrary to what many in the profession might feel. The fundamental nature of this function is the same and, therefore, consciously including health in our architectural mandates is a natural extension of what has been occurring organically for millennia.

Signage is only the most obvious way to frame an architectural situation. The full scope for architects is vast.

3.8 Reference Point Shifts

The last set of examples we discuss leads to a fascinating theory of transitional spaces in architecture.

There are many different types of transitions such as thresholds, porches, foyers, lobbies, passages connecting spaces in interiors, and so on. Each leads users from one space to another. Owing to the growing density of urbanization and the consequent reduction in apartment and office sizes, modernism and other styles following it have often been forced to do away with transitions. This has led to a new aesthetic in some cases where what might have been a passage leading to a living room has been absorbed into the living room to make it larger. This kind of subtle change in spaces is evident when one compares older apartments with newer ones in cities like New York. The former typically have smaller spaces with connecting passages and the latter have contiguous rooms with at most a hint of a transitional space. This does give modern apartments larger spaces, sometimes even stunning ones, but they come with a cost as we will soon see.

Instead of calling upon Phil, we will consider a whole set of examples together at a slightly more abstract level by isolating the key features of a transition, whatever particular form it might take. Whether it is a threshold that you step into before entering a house or a foyer inside a home where you hang your coat or a lobby in a building with a reception or a passage you walk along before entering a living or dining room or it is one of countless

Figure 3.24 A threshold

Figure 3.25 A transition to a living room

other types of transitions, its essence lies in allowing the person to enter the main space in two stages.

Rather than a sudden and immediate entry into what may be a grander space, there is time to prepare oneself for the experience. All architects know this and so do many others. This transitional time is made possible via a transitional *space* and in traditional buildings going back to classical times such time to ready oneself was always available. The alternative is a little like getting the main course in a big or small meal right away. To be sure the designer may sometimes be able to deliver a larger primary space

Figure 3.26 The living room viewed after the transition

by doing away with the transitional secondary space. This could make the main experience more impactful. But prospect theory suggests that even when this kind of tradeoff is possible the overall experience is generally less satisfying.

Consider the *S* curve of prospect theory in Figure 3.27. As before the *X*-axis shows gains on the positive side and losses on the negative side with respect to a reference point of 0 shown as a dot at the origin. Plotted against each gain or loss is a curve showing the value on the *Y*-axis that an agent derives from it. It is shaped like an *S*, being concave on the positive side and convex on the negative side.

To start, suppose there is no transition to the primary space. The experience of entering it can be modeled as a gain of 100 units starting from a reference of 0. For this gain of 100, the value we get is marked by a dot at (100, 80). This is straightforward to see visually on the graph. It expresses quantitatively the depth or richness of the experience.

Now imagine that the available area is divided differently into a primary space and a transitional secondary space. What happens in this instance is that the person first enters the transitional space and has a *smaller* preparatory experience, a kind of propaedeutic or introduction. Let's suppose this foreshadowing experience is a gain of 30 units. Its value on the *S* curve is

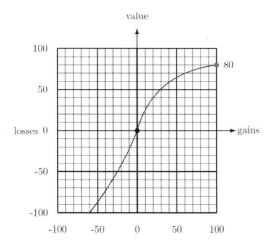

Figure 3.27 Value without transition

then 50 as can be seen from Figure 3.28 where the point is marked by a second dot at (30, 50).

As the person moves through the initial space, his reference point *shifts* from (0, 0) to (30, 50). That is, it shifts from the first dot to the second dot just mentioned. This happens because the experience of this first stage puts him at a higher level of satisfaction and he now measures the gains and losses of new experiences from this higher level.

This in turn leads him to have a whole new *S* curve at the new reference point which has the same shape as before. (The earlier *S* curve now drops out of the picture but is retained as a dotted line for the sake of clarity.) When he enters the primary space, his gains are measured from this new reference point. Another 100 units of gains are added (as the gain provided by the primary space remains the same) and this leads to an enhanced value of 130 units shown by a dot at (130, 130) as opposed to the earlier 80 units. This is because the new *S* curve starts off at a higher level after the person has already had a positive introductory experience in the transitional space.

Obviously, the dot at (130, 130) is much higher than the dot at (100, 80) and represents a significantly heightened experience. In other words, what prospect theory suggests is that having a transition generally yields greater satisfaction to a user because it is a compounded two-stage experience with a *shift of reference point* in between. The big experience piggybacks on the smaller one and so the user ascends to a higher level of impact.

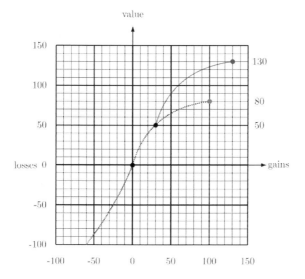

Figure 3.28 Value with transition

This can be expressed through equations as follows:

value(initial reference point)   = 0
value(new reference point after transition) = 50
value(primary space without transition)   = 80
value(primary space with transition)   = 130

This richer experience based on transitions is inseparable from its positive effects on our health. Negative experiences could also be contemplated by making a passage to something unpleasant seem dark and disquieting. More importantly, we should see clearly how architectural experience tends to merge with its effects on health and therefore how the Vitruvian triad involves overlapping dimensions rather than independent ones. From the point of view of health at least, one could claim that it is better to have transitions where it is feasible to have them.

It is worth pausing and reflecting on how neat and simple this explanation is and how it provides a *theory* of transitions of quite broad scope as it encompasses a wide variety of such spaces. We broke up the total gain of 130 into an initial gain of 30 followed by another gain of 100. After the first gain, the reference point shifts to a higher intermediate level taking the S curve to a new level with it. And this allows the user to extract a greater value from the second space. This piggybacking, or standing on the shoulders of a giant or a dwarf, whichever way you think of it, is what makes it possible. Notably, rational choice theory has no such devices that allow one to explain this phenomenon because it deals directly with the absolute benefits and costs of an experience rather than with relative values.

We have described this process in terms of experience. But note that prospect theory and its apparatus apply to choices and actions, not to experience as such. Theoretically speaking, it is possible to extend the concept of reference points and something like an S curve to experience itself. Instead of two stages of choices and actions, we would just have two stages of experience and the concomitant shift of reference point we have described. This could be thought of as an extension of prospect theory to situations beyond those it was meant to address.

One drawback of such a passive account of what happens when we pass through a transitional space is that the theory predicts it is inevitable and always occurs. This does not seem right. We often transit spaces without a deeper experience. This is why phenomenological theories also err when they attempt such explanations because they claim that experience is largely something that happens to us and so they cannot account for differences in experiences that depend on agents being active shapers of their experience. Nevertheless, this extension of prospect theory is not a bad account because it genuinely explains and does not merely describe the change as phenomenological accounts do. It lays bare the underlying mechanism responsible: a shift of reference point.

To apply prospect theory proper to this situation, the two experiences we have identified need to be related to two choice problems or equivalently to two meanings. One arises when there is no transition and the other arises when there is a transition. What, therefore, is the meaning of a space with or without a transition? This requires us to think of these architectural elements in terms of alternative actions the agent may choose.

What happens is this: the user enters a primary space with or without a transition. In this sort of situation, the only relevant actions other than simply walking are mental ones. One way of naming them is to say they are being mindful or not. That is, choices = {*be mindful, ignore*} or, even more simply, choices = {*notice, ignore*}. Sometimes users will have the leisure and will prefer to notice their ambient environment and at other times they will simply ignore what is happening around them as they may be preoccupied with other thoughts. In the former case, they will have the more acute and heightened experience; in the latter, they will not.

As we have done before, the meanings are identified with the cho[ice] problems induced by the spaces. Choice problems are the set of choi[ce] paired with the corresponding preferences.

We can therefore write:

> meaning of space without transition = ({*notice, ignore*}, {*notice ignore*})
>
> meaning of space with transition = ({*notice, ignore*}, {*notice* > *ignor*[e]}

Interestingly, the two meanings are the same because even when there is [no] transition it still pays to be mindful of one's surroundings. Additionally, [this] applies to all users as it is generally true that noticing is preferred, other thi[ng]s being equal. Recall that we discussed our everyday surroundings in the [fir]st chapter and how it is difficult but rewarding to become aware of them and [th]at they possess a fascinating structure capable of endless elaboration.

We have used the same definition of meaning here but this time w[ith] slight differences. This shows that the theoretical machinery at our disp[os]al is versatile and can adapt to different circumstances. We can go on thus

> space without transition → meaning → *notice* → rich experience: 80 units
>
> space with transition → meaning → *notice* → richer experience: 130 units

As a result of the two meanings being the same, the action that ensu[e]s is also the same: to notice the spaces with or without a transition. But wh[e]n a transition is present, the experience is further heightened than when [t]here isn't. In one case, its value is 80 units, in another its value is 130 units. One way of putting this is to say that qualitatively the two meanings are the [s]ame but quantitatively they are different. Since this applies to all users, it al[l]ows us to make a more general statement from an architectural viewpoint:

> meaning of space = C = ({*with transition, without transition*}, {*with transition* > *without transition*})

This is of course true only when no extraneous matters intervene. It r[e]pre-sents something like the central theorem of our account of transitions. This is not just a metaphorical way of speaking as the following statement o[f] this theorem shows.

Theorem 3.1. *Other things being equal, when a user is mindful of his surroundings, a space with a transition affords a more heightened po[s]itive or negative experience when the user is entering it than one without.*

The argument above leading to this statement is then the *proof* of the theorem.

One caveat is in order. To the original gain of 100 obtained from the primary space without a transition we added a further transitional gain of 30. Since the area available to the architect is often the same in many situations, the primary space would become smaller as some of it would be taken up by the transition. That is, its gain ought to be reduced from 100 to, say, 60. This is quite true but we did it this way to keep the calculations easy and the theory simple to grasp. Now that the main ideas are clear, it is straightforward to make the primary gain smaller and see what happens with a transition to this smaller primary space.

Take a look at Figure 3.29. First, the total gain is 30 + 60 = 90. The value derived from a gain of 90 is then shown by the dot at (90, 120). The value drops a little from the earlier 130 as we would expect but it is still 120, significantly more than the earlier 80. This implies that even in those circumstances where the architect cannot simply add a transition to a fixed primary space but has to carve up the primary space into two parts—a smaller transition and a relatively larger primary space—the theorem still holds.

We can display the relevant equation for this situation as well.

value (initial reference point)   = 0
value (new reference point after transition)   = 50
value (larger primary space without transition) = 80
value (smaller primary space with transition)   = 120

Looking back, our analysis may be expressed thus: judiciously placed *discontinuities* are desirable even if a given space has to be reduced *when assessed from the point of view of entering the primary space*. The italicized part of this statement is very important. The theorem does *not* compare what happens overall. For example, if an apartment is provided a transitional passage to a living room by making the latter smaller then it may happen that the time spent in the living room is less enjoyable. Our theorem only applies to the experience of entering the relevant space. But it is an interesting insight nonetheless.

If reference points did not shift, indeed if there were no reference points as there aren't in utility theory then the original S curve would be the one that dictates what values are experienced by slightly extending it in Figure 3.29. In the case where the primary space does not need to be reduced, it can be seen from the graph that a gain of 30 + 100 = 130 would yield just a little over 80, say 82 at most, and in the case where the primary space does need to be reduced, a gain of 30 + 60 = 90 would yield a little less than 80, say about 78. This is because the curve is almost flat or horizontal. In other

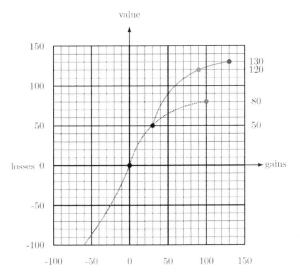

Figure 3.29 Value with transition to smaller space

words, if human beings were as utility theory describes them and evaluated absolute states of affairs, they would be more or less indifferent between entering a space with a transition and without. It is because of the way we actually are that is better captured by prospect theory that we judge things relative to reference points and when these shift they give rise to new phenomena and new explanations.

Our final observation is that this theorem applies only when discontinuities occur. Passing through a transitional space before entering a primary space involves such a discontinuity because architectural devices generally demarcate the separate spaces visually or otherwise. If this switch between two types of spaces did not occur, if the passage had been more or less continuous, then the reference point would not shift and the result would not apply. In such cases, some other principle like nonlinearity or anchoring could be relevant. This is a delicate point as it may not always be crystal clear whether there is a sufficient break between two types of experience and, therefore, whether a shift in reference point would occur.

3.9 An Overview of the Architectural Problem

In this chapter and the previous one, we have described a long list of "principles" that provide insights into both rational and irrational behavior and used them to explain and predict how appropriate architectural interventions can nudge people to adopt healthy actions more often than not. What sense can the architect make of this slightly bewildering array? How best to use them in her practice? How can she become a choice architect?

Perhaps the most important step she can take is to fully incorporate health and wellness into the Vitruvian triad, into her very conception of what architecture fundamentally is, rather than thinking of these functions as external afterthoughts as the profession does today. The deep reason for this, as we have been saying, is that there just is no neutral architecture. In other words, health and wellness are already part of utility, firmness, and beauty whether one likes it or not. The only choice an architect has is to acknowledge this brute fact or not.

The amazing thing is that once she admits this larger conception, once she embraces it, the field itself and all its spaces and elements at so many different levels, both from the distant past and the near present, appear in a radically different light. Their *meanings* change. It is a little like enacting a Copernican revolution where the external world remains what it is, only our fresh conception of it makes everything fit in simple and sensible ways unlike the awkward epicycles of Ptolemaic and pre-Copernican astronomy. Health and wellness become an inextricable and ineluctable part of architecture. Just as a well-designed space has an aesthetic potential so it inevitably also has a salubrious potential.

After this first conceptual transformation occurs, the second step is to rethink the nature of architectural meaning not so much by giving up existing "aesthetic" accounts but by adding to them the subjective, psychological, highly variable, and constantly changing framework of *choice problems* that we have proposed.

Remember that we started with a schema that is common to most approaches to architecturally induced wellness:

elements in the built environment → human experience → positive or negative effects on health

Usually the middle term is addressed holistically and descriptively but we broke it down into:

built environment → [(choices, preferences) → action] → effects on health

And this gave us our new definition of architectural meaning as a choice problem:

meaning of built environment = (choices, preferences) = C

We reinserted this new understanding of meaning into the schema to arrive at a synthesis of objective and subjective factors in the interaction between the built form and people:

built environment → meaning → action → effects on health

or equivalently:

built environment → choice problem → action → effects on health

Once we had these basic lineaments of our approach, we dug deeper into the endless variety of choice problems that arise when we encounter the built world. These can be classified into different types of actions as shown in Figure 3.30. Consistent rationality involves benefits and costs. Inconsistent rationality seems to subsume just the one principle of relativity. Irrational actions allow many more which we group in two separate figures as there are too many to fit in one. Figure 3.31 includes the first four biases we dealt with, all recast in terms of action and choice. Figure 3.32 deals with the next four including the more general meta-principle of framing and the mini theory of transitions we developed under the rubric of *reference point shifts*.

At the bottom of all three trees we've listed some of the examples we considered as applications of the various behavioral principles. Each principle was used to *explain* and *predict* how these particular architectural environments would work in having a positive or negative effect on our health. This is one of the key distinguishing features of our theory, that it provides a set of *mechanisms* for certain kinds of architectural semiosis. It does not

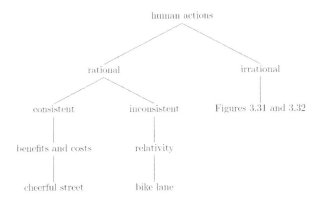

Figure 3.30 Types of human actions with architectural examples

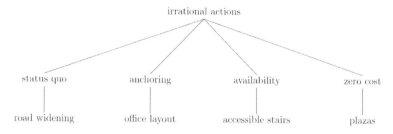

Figure 3.31 Types of irrational actions with architectural examples

Figure 3.32 Types of irrational actions with architectural examples

simply assert that this design element conveys that (subjective) meaning. It shows *how* and *why*.

This classification and our treatment in chapters 2 and 3 is not meant to be exhaustive. There could well be phenomena and principles we have left out and new ones might be uncovered. The extension to other architectural possibilities also beckons and it is up to the community of architects to uncover these. All these items fall under human action ultimately and so partly constitute choice problems and therefore meaning and interpretation.

It is these trees and the reasoning underlying them that the architect must familiarize herself with if she wishes to adopt the framework. As with the details of any such new picture, this one requires patient and sometimes intricate thought and assimilation if it is to be correctly and, in the end, effortlessly applied to new projects. We don't believe our economic and psychological approach is too outré or too difficult to become mainstream. As Kahneman has often emphasized in his books and papers, the ideas at the level we have introduced them, without any uncertainty in the situations we have considered, are quite simple and intuitive if one is open to noticing actual rather than imagined behavior. This receptivity combined with creativity of a high order led to the ideas of behavioral economics and it is the same combination of reality and innovation that is demanded of architects.

The most complex analytical step toward becoming a choice architect is the third and final one. What we have presented in the last two chapters is a collection of abstracted fragments of architectural scenarios to illustrate the operation of one principle or another. In an actual project, both the parts and the whole matter and our architect has to be careful about understanding the interactions of all these principles in an architectural whole, however small or large her undertaking. At this more comprehensive level, the science we have developed shades off into art and intuition and leaps of faith because concrete reality presents too vast a scope to encompass in a practical way. It is possible that one day some of this may be captured in algorithms that do some of this minute modeling for us, but until then the translation of theory into practice must remain part science and part art, which is the very nature of architecture itself.

To sum up, the architectural problem as we have been describing it involves three broad steps:

1. Acquiring a deep appreciation of how health and wellness fit seamlessly into architecture by reconceptualizing the form and content of the Vitruvian triad.
2. Understanding the new connection between meaning, choice, and action as compactly encapsulated by the three trees based on the insights of rational choice theory and behavioral economics.
3. Connecting the parts with each other and with the whole, what may be called the mereology of design, by combining science and art, which brings us back to the essence of architecture.

As we have called the architect who accepts such a program a choice architect, we dub the theory we are offering *choice architecture*.

Notes

1 Kahneman (2011, p. 122).
2 Anchoring also works via a different, more conscious mechanism of insufficient adjustment but this is less relevant for us.
3 Thaler and Sunstein (2008, p. 24).
4 Thaler and Sunstein (2008, p. 71).
5 Kahneman (2011, pp. 53–54).
6 Kahneman (2011).
7 Thaler and Sunstein (2008, p. 3).
8 Kahneman (2011, Chapter 12).

9   Thaler and Sunstein (2008, pp. 1–4).
10 Ariely (2008, Chapter 3).
11 Ariely (2008, pp. 58–59).
12 William Whyte (2001).
13 There are two kinds of nonlinearity: one refers to the concept we will be exploring and the other involves uncertain situations which we will not be dealing with in this book.
14 Kahneman (2011, pp. 272–277).
15 Kahneman (2011, pp. 272–277).
16 Tversky and Kahneman (1981).
17 Kahneman (2011, pp. 156–165).
18 Arrow (1982).

4 Reflecting on Choice Architecture

We started this book with the inescapability of everyday architectural influence. We have tried to show that it has a very rich structure although we have just scratched the surface in our use of economic and psychological ideas and also with regard to the range of architectural examples considered. We hope that this novel application of the seminal ideas of rational and irrational choice theory and the connection to a different way of looking at meaning will spur others to continue to develop *choice architecture*. In this concluding chapter, we offer a few reflections on the theory and how it transforms our perception of architecture.

4.1 Architecture Is Not a Tree

Over the course of the preceding chapters, we have said that when architecture and health are linked in the new way we are suggesting the classic and time-honored Vitruvian triad itself appears in a new light. To explain this change clearly, we introduce it step by step.

Vitruvius probably never intended his classification of architecture into utility, firmness, and beauty to be taken as a rigid mutually exclusive and collectively exhaustive partition of the field. But these components are often treated as separate categories. This tree-like conception is represented in Figure 4.1.

In this figure, architecture occupies the top parent node and utility, firmness, and beauty the three bottom child nodes. The top node is at a higher *level* and the bottom nodes are at a lower level and the structure is a hierarchical one. The idea is that architecture as a whole can be divided into a functional aspect, a structural aspect, and an aesthetic aspect. We might also say that architecture *expresses* or *causes* these three components to come about. For example, as an architectural element, a doorway has these three aspects or causes them to appear. It allows passage through it which is a function, it is made up of physical materials assembled in a structure, and it inevitably looks pleasing or not which belongs to the realm of aesthetics. So this tree-like conception applies not just to the field as a whole but also to its parts as shown in Figure 4.2.

This representation is called a tree partly because every aspect of a doorway or any other architectural element can be identified as belonging to exactly one of the categories of utility, firmness, or beauty. The fact that a door allows passage through it belongs only to utility, the fact that it is made up of materials combined in a certain way belongs only to firmness, and the fact that it is pleasant to behold belongs only to beauty. In other words, utility, firmness, and beauty are *distinct* just as black and white are distinct.

Our interest is in connecting architecture and its three components to wellness. Is there a way to place the latter somewhere in these figures? Should it be conceived as a type of function as pictured in Figure 4.3?

This is what we suggested in the opening paragraph of Chapter 2 and, indeed, this is how it is seen conventionally by architects.

The way to interpret Figure 4.3 is that wellness is a *consequence* or *effect* of the functional component of architecture. Put differently, architecture *causes* or *creates* wellness via its functional aspect. This is nothing but a different way of expressing our old schema:

architectural element → meaning → action → wellness

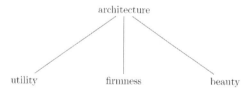

Figure 4.1 The Vitruvian triad

Figure 4.2 The Vitruvian triad applied to doorways

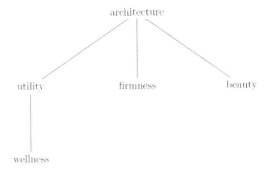

Figure 4.3 The Vitruvian triad showing wellness as a kind of function

Indeed, we can insert *utility* into this schema to show exactly how an element might have a wellness effect via its utility component.

architectural element → utility → meaning → action → wellness

This mainstream picture allows wellness to be treated as *expendable* and as unconnected with other aspects of the field because any architectural part and the relevant whole fulfill many functions, not all of which may matter equally, so it is up to the architect to decide whether to attend to their wellness effects or not.

As the book progressed, we began to opt for a more complex picture with all three components of architecture playing a role in bringing about wellness, not just utility. These multiple rubrics of health are depicted in Figure 4.4.

A tree requires that every child node has just one parent node, that is, every node is linked to just one node above it, so that there is a unique path from any bottom node to the top node. But the wellness node has *three* parent nodes. This makes architecture into something other than a tree just as the architect and design theorist Christopher Alexander pointed out that a city is not a tree.[1] Incidentally, since wellness actually arises from meaning according to our framework of interpretation, we really should be presenting this as shown in Figure 4.5.

Now, the Copernican revolution we mentioned, the reconceptualization of the form and content of the Vitruvian triad, is beginning to emerge. Meaning and wellness have become more central as they are not simply one function among many, but they are also structural and aesthetic effects

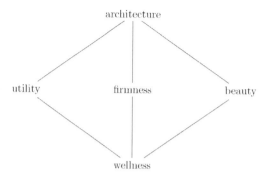

Figure 4.4 The Vitruvian triad showing architecture is not a tree

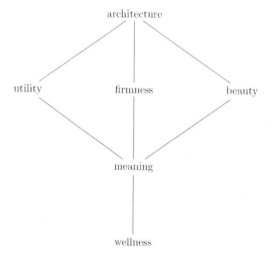

Figure 4.5 The Vitruvian triad with meaning

of architectural parts and wholes such as a doorway or a whole building or even a city. This very same structure can also be presented via the following three schemata:

architectural element → utility → meaning → action → wellness
architectural element → firmness → meaning → action → wellness
architectural element → beauty → meaning → action → wellness

There are three schemata now rather than one because architecture has three separate components. The understanding here is that an element has some aspects that work via utility, others via firmness, and yet others via beauty, each of which first affects meaning and then wellness.

But the two diagrams in Figures 4.4 and 4.5 nevertheless allow us to separate the sources of meaning and wellness into the three components of utility, firmness, and beauty in a mutually exclusive way. That is, the form and content of the triad have been changed into something different from a tree but not yet wholly transformed.

What we have been alluding to in fact is that these nodes *overlap* and cannot be cleanly separated into distinct categories. How should this partial fusion be imagined? This is a complex visual demand as two independent requirements must be included in one picture: the overlapping categories and the hierarchical levels of a tree from a parent to its child nodes and so on. There is no easy way to do this so we will focus just on the attribute of overlapping components.

The kind of *imbricated* picture of architecture we are positing is portrayed in Figure 4.6. The three nodes of utility, firmness, and beauty have now become three overlapping circles. We have also placed meaning in their intersection but that placement has to be interpreted with caution. Remember that meaning is one level down from utility, firmness, and beauty in Figure 4.5 although our Venn diagram shows them at the same flattened

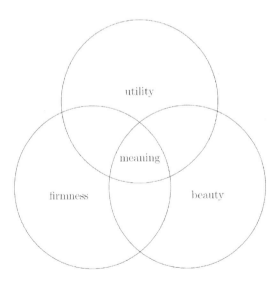

Figure 4.6 The overlapping Vitruvian triad with meaning

level. Not only this, the architectural element which occupied the top node is completely missing. So we have to carefully interpret this diagram as conveying that meaning is an effect of some architectural element via utility, firmness, and beauty. As we have flattened the hierarchy, we can further flatten it and go directly to wellness in Figure 4.7 as that is our ultimate goal.

These two pictures, simple as they are, make clear that the three components of utility, firmness, and beauty are not fully isolable but blend with each other and, moreover, that meaning and wellness *are caused by* their fused intersection. What these diagrams convey is that meaning and wellness are a result of often hard-to-separate aspects of architecture where utility, firmness, and beauty may well merge in ineffable ways. Is *this* effect on health a result of *that* aspect of utility or *that* aspect of firmness or *that* aspect of beauty? It can be difficult to say.

This is not yet the final story. It is still an intermediate step. All we have captured so far is the merging of the Vitruvian triad, but we are not finished with meaning and wellness.

To be fully accurate, meaning and wellness do not belong only in the intersection of the three circles. They can appear anywhere in the enclosed area, sometimes arising purely out of one of the three components, sometimes from any two of them, and only sometimes from all three. All these

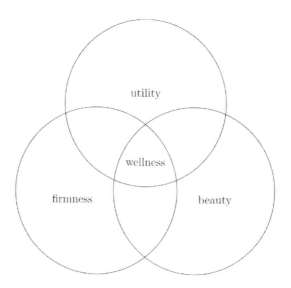

Figure 4.7 The overlapping Vitruvian triad with wellness

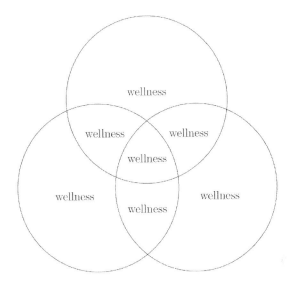

Figure 4.8 The overlapping Vitruvian triad with meaning and wellness everywhere

seven cases are shown in Figure 4.8. Again, keep in mind that in this flattened picture, we cannot show that wellness is one level down from and an effect of utility, firmness, and beauty.

Because these effects occur everywhere (within the three circles), there is no neutral architecture. No matter what an architect does, it will have a meaning and will affect a user's health in good ways or bad. For example, the adequacy of lighting in an interior or exterior is a pure function that signifies safety and makes the relevant space safe, a positive effect. On the other hand, inadequate lighting has the opposite effect. To drive home the ubiquity of the connection to wellness, we place the various architectural examples we have considered so far in Figure 4.9.

In Figure 4.8, utility, firmness, and beauty *cause* or *create* wellness which is an *effect*. In Figure 4.9, the various architectural elements *cause* or *create* utility, firmness, and beauty just as a doorway *has* functional, structural, and aesthetic effects. So the way to understand the two figures differs because in the first wellness is an effect and in the second the elements are a cause. We clarify this in two ways: by showing the terms *utility*, *firmness*, and *beauty* as resulting from the bike lane and the office layout and the plaza respectively in Figure 4.9 and by re-presenting the three schemata above as

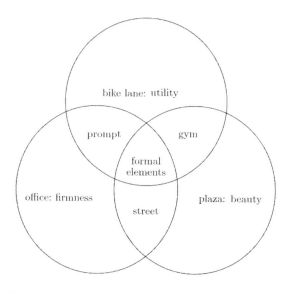

Figure 4.9 The overlapping Vitruvian triad with wellness examples everywhere

one merged schema with "utility/firmness/beauty" to be read as "utility and/
or firmness and/or beauty":

architectural element → utility/firmness/beauty → meaning → action
→ wellness

This merged schema captures the whole sequence from initial cause to final
effect and makes clear how, for example, a bike lane or office layout or
plaza or stair prompt or street or gym or formal element has one or more
Vitruvian effects which have a meaning that affects our health in positive or
negative ways. These final pictures need some thought to be fully grasped
and should be related to Figures 3.30, 3.31, and 3.32 in the previous chapter.

Now, the Copernican transformation we have been referring to is fully
represented. It shows not only how meaning and wellness are *native* to
every part and whole of the field but also shows the field itself in a new
light. The conventional view of wellness as an afterthought, as not really
belonging to architecture proper has been overturned into its exact opposite where it is unavoidable and everywhere. Utility, firmness, and beauty
are themselves seen afresh and in more complex ways. At the close of the
last chapter we said that acquiring a deep appreciation of how health and

wellness fit seamlessly into architecture by reconceptualizing the form and content of the Vitruvian triad was the first step toward solving the architectural problem; now we hope this step has been fully clarified.

4.2 The Structure of Architectural Experience

As is evident from the choice-theoretic approach we have adopted toward both meaning and the link between architecture and health, we have abstracted from a more holistic conception of experience in the schema:

elements in the built environment → human experience → positive or negative effects on health

and reduced it to:

experience: (choices, preferences) → action

As we noted earlier, when preferences are rational, they can be replaced by equivalent utility numbers, and when they are not, choice problems directly involve the numerical values of relative gains and losses—the counterparts of utilities in prospect theory. With some principles, such as anchoring and availability, we did not explicitly use either utility theory or prospect theory but something similar, either qualitative like preferences or quantitative like utility or value numbers, can nevertheless stand in for experience. That is, (choices, preferences) are generalized to choice problems C which can take a greater variety of forms than utility theory or prospect theory can encompass.

It is reasonable to have two concerns about this complex of procedures, especially in architecture. The first is narrower and asks whether this kind of structuring of experience is *too* reductive. The second is broader and raises the issue of whether such a scientific approach to architecture is too "positivistic" to address some of its central questions. These are large concerns and we can only offer a few observations about them here.

Even when we describe a phenomenon in ordinary language, we select aspects of it from the infinitude it presents. This, too, is a reduction of the original experience, say Phil's experience of the cheerful street, because words also fall short of its totality. So preferences or numbers are in this respect similar to words in that neither is able to capture the whole. This abstractive quality is perhaps the very nature of understanding, be it "scientific" or not.

But what the application of choice theory does is to uncover a precise structure in an aspect of experience that can support reasoning, understanding, empirical testing, and, especially, sharper conclusions in a way that words often cannot. We have seen this precision in action when we represented the overlapping dimensions of utility, firmness, and beauty through Venn diagrams, not to mention our analysis of architectural encounters via choice problems throughout. Those who prefer words or pictures or find themselves uncomfortable with such precision may well wonder whether this additional exactitude comes with a cost that somehow distorts the original experience. They may argue that words and pictures are often vague even though they can sometimes be used to craft very precise statements, and this vagueness is somehow reflective of the fact that Phil's experience, too, has no sharp boundaries. That is, both words and the reality being described are fuzzy and so of a piece in a way that mathematical language is not. That is why the latter may misrepresent in a way that the former may not. So while some reduction is necessary for understanding whatever type of language is used, such skeptics may feel choice theory goes too far in its precision and *falsifies* experience.

In such matters, the proof of the pudding is always in the eating. Certainly verbal and visual languages can be very powerful and we are well advised to use them in many circumstances such as this very discussion of the right way to approach experience in our architectural setting. But when there are precise structures to be grasped *in* the phenomena of interest, when these structures are not being externally imposed but internally drawn out or inferred, then we should not hesitate to use the language appropriate to them because in such cases the language *mirrors* the object and there is no falsification. In our situation, it happens to be the language of choice theory and whether it is true to architectural experience as it relates to health will be borne out by its further elaboration and empirical testing as we have been urging all along. Our claim is that the various choice problems Phil and Tom have experienced in the book accurately reflect reality. Science has been enormously successful in a variety of areas, even in architecture itself, and there is no a priori way to judge whether our method will succeed or not.

Having said this, it is extremely important to always keep the whole concrete architectural problem in mind and go back and forth between it and our abstract model of it. This is the only way to prevent the common error of scientism, which is to treat the phenomenon and its understanding as identical. Phil's architectural encounters are always a concrete whole and the choice problems he extracts from them are always only abstractions. So no theory should be extended indiscriminately beyond its legitimate area of application. Understanding of any kind is always *partial* because the objects of our understanding are always infinite.

To sum up our response to the first concern of reduction, we have seen that all understanding involves some reduction, and as long as choice theory is not arbitrarily foisted upon architectural experience, we are right to approach the latter with the former. The choice structures are there to be *found*; they are not brought in from outside. That is what can make a theory *true*.

To turn to the second issue of a possible mismatch between science and the broader ethical import of architecture, something many architects are rightly concerned about, we believe that the human species is fully a part of nature. There is no Cartesian mind-body dualism or radical culture-nature distinction. To us the notion that our minds are different from everything else in the entire universe seems implausible. Human values, too, emerge from history which is in the end just the story of human action and interaction.

These are no doubt controversial claims that continue to be debated, but we see the challenge as one of *housing* all the complexity of our species within a naturalizable, that is, ultimately a scientific framework. Part of this will be best served by being expressed through mathematics, which is just a language, part through ordinary verbal language, and part through other media including architecture. We think some of the early twentieth century critiques of "positivism" in particular misunderstood science as a much more circumscribed enterprise than it in fact is.[2] Scientists (and analytic philosophers) themselves understood their work too narrowly and contributed to this. As long as scientific activity is carried out with caution and sensitivity toward physical and social nature, it can be one of the surest ways to reveal partial truths about it. It is right for architecture to be ambitious, even utopian, and in this quest, science can be an indispensable aid. If approached properly, architecture can improve the health of the planet on a vast scale.

A related but less abstract matter is the worry about social engineering. Does choice architecture encourage a kind of manipulation of the innocent Phil? There are two points to make here. First, when we go to a restaurant, the food we are served is also never neutral. The chef could use fresher ingredients or not. Either way he will affect our health. It is the same with architecture. Our architect could serve up a cheerful street or depressing street. Knowing that the former has a positive effect and the latter a negative effect, she may as well choose to do Phil a good turn rather than not. Second, we are reasonably in control of what we order at a restaurant and we can always try to make the best of even a bad situation. In the same way, Phil is an autonomous agent and even though his architectural experience is structured for him, he is still free to make a choice. This may come at a cost of course, the cost of being overly vigilant about his actions. But it shows that the question of freedom versus social engineering involves nuance and tradeoffs rather than absolute black and white judgments. We have simply made the commonsense assumption in our approach that it is desirable for societies to expend resources to spread wellness and prevent illness.

4.3 A Few Cautionary Remarks

We have mentioned some pitfalls of using choice architecture throughout this text and we gather a few of them here.

Perhaps the most important of these is knowing when other things are equal and so can be ignored in an application. This is the *ceteris paribus* assumption. If Phil is habitually late for work, he is not going to walk no matter how attractive the street. Another aspect of this is that two architectural interventions may interact by contradicting each other and canceling their effects. In some circumstances, a bike lane can interfere with a street and they can nullify each other's inducements. So a holistic measure of the situation is required to ensure that each principle's intended action can be legitimately isolated.

We have used both utility theory and prospect theory but how does one know in advance which will apply? Related to this, how does one know which principle to use in a given situation? These are delicate questions and require making the right assumptions about the social context in which the environment is being designed. Part of this is acquiring the experience to know when fast intuitive thinking will dominate and when slow deliberation will occur. There is no shortcut.

Another real concern is whether in an actual project there will be so many variables, so much complexity that they make the problem intractable. Such multivariable problems have been tackled with modest success in many areas. For example, we are able to predict the weather with far better accuracy nowadays and likewise can manage all kinds of network flows such as airplane traffic and routing. Can choice architecture be married to such techniques where required so that some of it remains an art and but some of it becomes increasingly amenable to science and its algorithms?

A fourth pitfall is that we have focused almost entirely on positive uses of our irrationality, but irrationality can drive us to do negative things as much as positive ones. The status quo bias we discussed in Chapter 2 in Tom's case was seen to have a positive effect on his health in one pair of situations and a negative effect when the situations were reversed. Indeed, this is likely to always happen with status quo biases. Such negative occurrences can be present with the other principles as well, so we have to be careful about what kind of effect will prevail in the circumstances at hand.

Power and hierarchy in large and small settings can often foil the best of programs if they are innocent of the social situation. In the reimagining of Phil's office layout, the higher-ups could quash the better initiatives if they stand to lose too much. In such cases, rational discussion is perhaps the only way out but this is only possible on a small scale. Other things have to happen in society to make wider neutralizations of the unreasonable exercise of power possible.

The sixth critical dimension cannot be overemphasized. Sensitive observation and empirical testing of the hypotheses are a must. That will help to hone the theory in ways that cannot be anticipated. Some claims may have to be abandoned because what seemed like a plausible analogy does not carry over to an architectural setting. Or a principle that works in one kind of space may fail in another, suggesting conditions for its application that are at present undiscovered. Even a reorganization of the elements of choice theory can emerge from such scrutiny. For this a community of researchers and practitioners is required: architects, health professionals, and even economists.

Lastly, it is possible we have been too optimistic about the prospects for architecture's nudging people to adopt healthy choices. Such interventions are already being tried with limited success: pedestrian plazas and bike and bus lanes seem to cause traffic congestion and frustration, perhaps making life more pleasant for a small segment of society at the expense of many more who just want to get from *a* to *b*. It may be true that many of us lead lives of quiet desperation and marginal improvements to our health are a luxury we cannot afford. Our response to this very real issue is twofold. First, the very cautions we are urging may not always have been heeded in the desire to intervene. Has the whole situation really been kept in mind or has a decontextualized abstraction been allowed to determine the solution in such settings? When the full context is considered, it can of course turn out that no easy answer to the problem exists and compromises will be inevitable.

More broadly, the potential of architecture to transform society has to be articulated through patient and detailed analyses, not grand declamations. The result of such a cautiously optimistic approach is not going to be either-or but if-then, that is, it is not going to be black or white but provisional. If such and such conditions exist, then such and such consequences are likely to follow. Architecture must walk the middle path between the Scylla of a sweeping and unrealizable idealism and the Charybdis of a simplistic and shallow realism. As every architect knows, God is in the detail.

4.4 Uncertainty

A central feature of decision-making and, indeed, life that we have pointedly avoided in all the examples we have discussed is uncertainty. If Phil decides to walk one morning, his salubrious choice and the pleasant experience it partly constitutes may be marred by rain. Or Tom's plan to bike may be thwarted by unexpected congestion in the bike lane because too many neighbors opt to bike the same day. Phil's well-lit new office might reduce his fatigue but its new layout may not anchor him to playing tennis a particular evening because he develops a cold. And so on. Uncertainty is everywhere.

It is no coincidence that utility theory goes back to the eighteenth century,[3] only a century or so after probability theory was first formulated. Its subsequent elaboration and refinement in the twentieth century has led to a very elegant and mathematically sophisticated framework for considering *rational* choice in the face of uncertainty. And in the late 1970s Kahneman and Tversky developed their equally elegant prospect theory which deals with uncertain prospects and accommodates a fair bit of our *irrational* behavior as well. So both rational and irrational choice theory have been linked to probability from the very beginning.

We have limited our discussion of uncertainty so as to not introduce too many new ideas all at once and also because the relevant theories become much more complex. For those who are interested, a worthy challenge beckons. This is part of the reason why we said that everyday encounters with architecture have a fascinating structure capable of endless elaboration.

Uncertainty can come from many relevant directions. A number of principles can even accommodate probability *internally*. For example, anchoring may in fact be inherently probabilistic because its outcome—Phil's playing tennis—is not guaranteed. One might say there is an even chance or 50–50 chance of it succeeding. Or even if the stairs in Phil's office are attractive and accessible, he may sometimes take them and sometimes not in a random way. Thus, there can be internal ways such as these and external ways such as the ones above of bringing uncertainty into the framework.

In any case, even though we have confined our exploration to examples with certainty, we hope we have offered something to reflect on and audiences can take it where they will.

4.5 Utility and Meaning

We started with the pre-theoretical schema:

elements in the built environment → human experience → positive or negative effects on health

and ended with the theoretical schema:

architectural element → utility/firmness/beauty → choice problem → action → wellness

or equivalently:

architectural element → utility/firmness/beauty → meaning → action → wellness

By now, this causal picture should be thoroughly familiar. As we have seen, it allows us to rethink the Vitruvian triad of utility, firmness, and beauty in a way that relates health and wellness to all three overlapping components. It therefore enables us to conceive human well-being as an integral part of every architectural endeavor rather than as the afterthought it usually is.

Choice architecture has two parts: a new application of rational and irrational choice theory and a new way of seeing meaning. The choice theory part is the nuts and bolts *mechanism* our framework offers. The meaning part shows how this mechanism fits into architectural experience by identifying meaning with the choice structure the agent faces afresh with every architectural encounter—what we called the *choice problem.*

We have explained the choice theory aspect in some detail. One thing to notice is that the term "utility" appears both in rational choice theory and also in the Vitruvian triad. Is there a connection between these two uses of the same word? The latter use refers to the *function* served by one or more architectural elements. When functions are viewed broadly they include external behavior such as enabling passage through a transition as well as evoking internal feelings of anticipation and comfort when such passage occurs. The former choice-theoretic use of the term refers to positive and negative effects on the agent of a choice, its benefits and costs. So there are similarities and differences between the two uses. The similarities are that they both concern *effects* and the differences are that in one case these effects belong to architectural elements and in the other to a choice. But we have seen that choices are embedded in the surrounding architecture as much as they are in our human capacities and our societies—remember Phil's choosing between walking and taking the bus—so we can in fact say that the differences between the two are immaterial. This makes the two uses of "utility" *practically* the same. And since the relative *values* of prospect theory are just a cognate term for utilities in the context of a different theory, we can say the same of them as well. This is an unexpected and welcome convergence between architecture and choice theory, that both deal with utility in its broadest sense, and it reinforces the conviction expressed earlier that utility is equally an *intellectual* part of architecture as much as it is an obviously practical part. To paraphrase the artist Giorgio Morandi, *nothing is more theoretical than practice.*[4]

In developing the applications of choice theory, we have tried wherever possible to highlight second-order, relatively counterintuitive behaviors that are not obvious as opposed to something obvious like the effects of adequate lighting on our safety. This is part of what makes an enterprise a worthwhile *science.* Otherwise a collection of commonsense observations would suffice and, as we said, this has been the mainstay of the field of design and health with evidence-based design, human factor design, action research, and so on. Such a collection of data is very useful and can even be indispensable in developing a theory but without a theory to guide the collection of data, it is possible for the data to remain relatively mundane and unilluminating. But we, too, have just scratched the surface of this large terrain and a great deal more work of a theoretical and practical kind remains to be done.

This brings us to meaning which we have addressed fleetingly at best. We said at the outset that we were *stipulating* that the meaning of an architectural element was to be identified with the choice problem it induces. Was this stipulation arbitrary or does it square with meaning generally? What is meaning anyway? These questions are central to our project but we avoided them earlier to not interrupt Phil's (and Tom's) stories. We turn to them briefly and show how our stipulation flows from a larger and more encompassing view of meaning.

There are many kinds of things in the world. There are *individuals*[5] such as architraves and pediments, and thresholds and foyers, and even buildings and cities, not to mention chairs and tables. Each of these individuals has an infinite number of *properties* such as being colored and having a shape. And these individuals also stand in *relations* such as a chair being beside a table or a pediment being above an architrave or even a building being in a city. Complexes of these, individuals *having* properties or *standing in* relations, form *situations*, parts of the world we occupy as agents and move about in. Such an inventory is an *informational space*. All agents, whether ants or humans, carve up reality and create an informational space to navigate the world.

In carving up reality, one of the key things they do is *connect* two items of information such as, say, smoke and fire. When such a connection occurs with a certain *regularity*, that is, when it possesses a predictable *structure*, we call it a *meaning*. Indeed, we say that smoke *means* fire and, likewise, that a cheerful street *means* a certain kind of choice problem.

The built environment is full of such connections or meanings only some of which are choice problems. It is aesthetic meanings such as cultural references or evocations of the past, present, or future that interest most architects. But we can see that choice-related meanings and aesthetic meanings are of the same kind: they both depend on there being a suitably reliable *connection* between an architectural element and something else, either a choice problem or some other abstract idea. This is why our earlier stipulation wasn't arbitrary but flowed out of this larger conception of meaning.

In fact, science is nothing but trying to understand the multitude of these connections in reality. So science can be said to be *the search for meaning*, and choice architecture is just one instance of this.

4.6 The Inescapable Architecture of Everyday Life

As T. S. Eliot wrote, we have arrived "where we started. And know the place for the first time." It has always been a possibility for architecture to be bold symbolically and aesthetically and deliver outstanding but isolated achievements that introduce new meanings and new experiences of beauty into the public realm. This has largely been a story of architectural exceptionalism. Many have also attempted to alter the social fabric itself through utopian ideas and ideals but could not succeed without a clear understanding of the nature of the link between architecture and action.

In this book, we have tried to clarify this link through the prism of behavioral economics by offering a different strategy: to *see* and *feel* architecture through fresh eyes and senses and thereby to transform it from a singular and frozen music into a diverse, plural, and most importantly, *dynamic* and *interactive* set of influences teeming with life. We have shown through a *theoretical* approach that the potential of architecture for social effects is expressed in *two* ways, the first being the familiar mainstream path of a kind of monumentalism and grand gesture, and the second being the more quiet but perhaps more powerful path of a democratic universalism that exists in the smallest room and the largest city.

The choice problems architectural encounters generate in everyday settings are among the meanings Phil and Tom experience and their choices make the difference between wellness and illness. Choice architecture renders hard-to-see minute effects visible and shows that they add up through repetition and variation. In all this, each person emerges as an *active* agent who partly shapes his experience and chooses to be healthy through his fast or slow thinking. The earlier pictures of architecturally induced social outcomes were typically macroscopic; the picture we have drawn is microscopic because it reveals the *details* of the interaction between the individual and his environment. It is also cumulative and inescapable and can be extended to whole communities.

The mother who wondered about how being schooled in a rigid corridor-centric building without art or natural light could make a child bright, courageous, and well-rounded with an appreciation for beauty in life now has her answer: it generally cannot, but there are definite ways to change the design of buildings that can not only make the child physically healthy but can also mentally expose her to the full range of human possibility.

All of human action swims in this ambient architectural water of the fish in David Foster Wallace's parable.[6] The framework we have presented tries to grasp and lay bare the connection between architecture and life that humankind has experienced all along. To the extent we have succeeded, it will enable us to *understand* and *explain* how architecture affects life and therefore how it *can have* life itself.

Notes

1 Alexander (1965).
2 For example, Bernstein (1978), Dallmayr and McCarthy (1978).
3 Bernoulli (1738/1954).
4 Morandi's original statement was that nothing is more abstract than reality.
5 This philosophical term refers to individual objects of any kind, not just to people.
6 David Foster Wallace, convention speech to graduating class at Kenyon College, 2005.

Bibliography

Alexander, C. A city is not a tree. *Architectural Forum*, 122(1): 58–62, April 1965.

Allais, Maurice. Le comportement de l'homme rationnel devant le risque, critique des postulats et axiomes de l'École Americaine. *Econometrica*, 21: 503–546, 1953.

Almass, Ingerid Helsing. Nudges for a better architecture? *Arkitecktur N, The Norwegian Review of Architecture*, 5: 26–37, March 2013.

Ariely, Dan. *Predictably Irrational: The Hidden Forces That Shape Our Decisions*. HarperCollins, New York, 2008.

Arrow, Kenneth J. Risk perception in psychology and economics. *Economic Inquiry*, 20(1), 1982.

Bernoulli, D. Exposition of a new theory of the measurement of risk. *Econometrica*, 22: 23–36, 1738/1954.

Bernstein, Richard J. *The Restructuring of Social and Political Theory*. University of Pennsylvania Press, Philadelphia, PA, 1978.

Casey, Edward. *Getting Back Into Place: Toward a Renewed Understanding of the Place-World*. Indiana University Press, Bloomington, IN, second edition, 2009.

Currie, John Michael. *The Fourth Factor: A Historical Perspective on Architecture and Medicine*. American Institute of Architects, Washington DC, 2007.

Dallmayr, Fred R. and Thomas A. McCarthy, editors. *Understanding and Social Inquiry*. University of Notre Dame Press, Notre Dame, IN, 1978.

Gibson, J. J. *The Ecological Approach to Visual Perception*. Lawrence Erlbaum Associates, Hillsdale, NJ, 1979.

Kahneman, Daniel. *Thinking, Fast and Slow*. Farrar, Straus and Giroux, New York, 2011.

Kahneman, Daniel and Amos Tversky. Prospect theory: An analysis of decision under risk. *Econometrica*, 47(2): 263–291, March 1979.

Kahneman, Daniel and Amos Tversky. Choices, values, and frames. In Daniel Kahneman and Amos Tversky, editors, *Choices, Values, and Frames*, pages 1–16. Cambridge University Press, Russell Sage Foundation, New York, 2000.

Kahneman, Daniel, Paul Slovic, and Amos Tversky, editors. *Judgement Under Uncertainty: Heuristics and Biases*. Cambridge University Press, Cambridge, 1982.

Maier, J. A., G. M. Fadel, and D. G. Battisto. An affordance-based approach to architectural theory, design, and practice. *Design Studies*, 30(4): 393–414, 2009.

Michaels, Claire F. and Claudia Carello. *Direct Perception*. Prentice-Hall, New York, 1981.

Parikh, Avani. *Behavior, Design, and Wellness*. Poster exhibited at Design and Health: Seventh World Congress and Exhibition, Boston, 2011.

Pevsner, Nikolaus. *An Outline of European Architecture*. Penguin Books, London, seventh edition, 1943/1990.

Rush, Fred. *On Architecture*. Routledge, New York, 2009.

Schmidt, Karsten. When architecture meets nudging. *iNudgeyou*, September 26, 2012. www.inudgeyou.com/archives/2577.

Shirazi, M. Reza. *Towards An Articulated Phenomenological Interpretation of Architecture: Phenomenal Phenomenology*. Routledge, New York, 2014.

Simon, Herbert A. A behavioral model of rational choice. *Quarterly Journal of Economics*, 69: 99–118, 1955.

Simon, Herbert A. Rational choice and the structure of the environment. *Psychological Review*, 63: 129–138, 1956.

Spiegelberg, Herbert. *The Phenomenological Movement: A Historical Introduction*. Springer, Berlin, 1981.

Techau, David, Ceridwen Owen, Douglas Paton, and Roger Fay. Buildings, Brains and Behavior. *World Health Design*, 24–37, January 2016.

Thaler, R. H. and C. R. Sunstein. *Nudge: Improving Decisions About Health, Wealth, and Happiness*. Yale University Press, New Haven, CT, 2008.

Tversky, Amos and Daniel Kahneman. The framing of decisions and the psychology of choice. *Science*, 211(4481): 453–458, January 1981.

Tversky, Amos and Daniel Kahneman. Loss aversion in riskless choice: A reference-dependent model. In Daniel Kahneman and Amos Tversky, editors, *Choices, Values, and Frames*, pages 143–158. Cambridge University Press, Russell Sage Foundation, New York, 2000. Originally published in *The Quarterly Journal of Economics*, 106(4): 1039–61, 1991.

Whyte, William H. *The Social Life of Small Urban Spaces*. Project for Public Spaces, New York, 2001.

Zaitchik, Amanda. Applying Gibson's theory of affordances to interior design. In Jeremy Wells and Elefterios Pavlides, editors, *Proceedings of the 44th Annual Conference of the Environmental Design Research Association*, pages 170–178, 2013.

Zeisel, John. *Inquiry by Design*. W. W. Norton, New York, 2006.

Index